Love you
*Public policy for
intergenerational
wellbeing*

This is a book we need – now. Weaving international research, philosophic thought, and leadership experience spanning public and private sectors, and grounded with a strong sense of being a 'human' citizen, Girol Karacaoglu beautifully reveals the limitations of our current government and public service settings and reconnects us to our simple shared human story. He uses this simplicity and clarity to throw light on our complex challenges and helps illuminate the direction we need to head. A must read for anyone wanting to be of service to the public and enhance our collective wellbeing.

> – **David Hanna**, CLD Influencing and Practice Lead, Inspiring Communities

A great contribution to the growing wellbeing and public policy field and one that is properly holistic. This serious consideration of intergenerational impacts of policy making and practical ways of making really difficult prioritisation decisions in the contested space of public policy moves the field forward in a robust and relevant way. Rich and highly relevant to the challenges we are facing.

> – **Nancy Hey**, Executive Director, What Works Wellbeing

Love you
Public policy for intergenerational wellbeing

Girol Karacaoglu

TUWHIRI

Wellington
Aotearoa New Zealand

First published 2021

The Tuwhiri Project
PO Box 6626 Wellington 6141
Aotearoa New Zealand
www.tuwhiri.nz

© Girol Karacaoglu
This work is licensed under a Creative Commons Attribution-NonCommercial-ShareAlike 4.0 International License

ISBN: 978-0-473-55789-8

A catalogue record for this book is available from the National Library of New Zealand

Kei te pātengi raraunga o Te Puna Mātauranga o Aotearoa te whakarārangi o tēnei pukapuka

Book design: John Houston
Cover design: minimum graphics
Set in Fira Sans and IBM Plex Serif

10 9 8 7 6 5 4 3 2 1

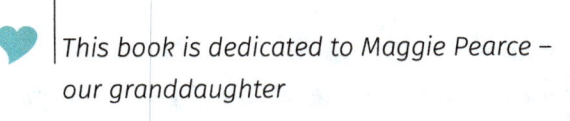 *This book is dedicated to Maggie Pearce – our granddaughter*

Also by Girol Karacaoglu

Intergenerational wellbeing and public policy – an integrated environmental, social, and economic framework (2019) – with Anita King and Jacek B Krawczyk

Public policy and governance frontiers in New Zealand (2020) – edited with Evan Berman

Social policy practice and processes in Aotearoa New Zealand (2021) – edited with Graham Hassall

Contents

	Foreword	ix
	Preface	xxv
1.	Introduction	1
2.	Wellbeing and a radically different policy approach	15
3.	Public policy in a radically different world	25
4.	Resilience as a platform for sustained prosperity	39
5.	Governing for intergenerational wellbeing	61
6.	Inclusive processes required for sustained wellbeing	83
7.	How do we know if wellbeing policy is effective?	101
8.	What would I prioritise and why?	115
9.	Living well – circular wellbeing	131
10.	Epilogue: Covid-19 – wellbeing-focused policy response	133
	Appendix 1: Evidence – institutions and wellbeing	143
	Appendix 2: Evidence – broader impacts of opportunity on wellbeing	147
	References	157
	About the author	175
	The Nest Collective	178
	About Tuwhiri	179

Foreword
The opening of minds towards wellbeing

Robert H. Wade, professor of global political economy at the London School of Economics

Deep society-wide crises – like depressions, world wars, pandemics – tend to produce new economic thinking. 2020 has familiarised many millions with trauma and loss. But it has also shaken the hold of the conservative economic doctrine – or moral frame – which has dominated economic policy making across the capitalist world for the past four decades, no less, as though the very definition of common sense.

The conservative moral frame
The doctrine feeds a whole cultural ecosystem based on mistrust of government and the idea of tax-as-theft – as in politicians' everyday talk of 'spending taxpayers' money' and the ubiquitous use of the phrase 'tax burden'. The implication is that how much you earn is what you deserve from hard work and righteousness, and the tax you pay is taken from what is rightfully yours. People who are not earning a living are not disciplined, therefore deserve their poverty. The public and private sectors have mostly opposed interests. 'Government intervention', even for good social causes, comes at the cost of efficiency and growth. The costs of 'government failure' are generally higher than the costs of 'market failure'. Low taxes and low public debt make for an economically moral society, which gives the wealthy legitimation for their good fortune.

What is the root economic idea behind this mindset? The world economy should be integrated by the free flow of capital, which implies that property rights over the use of capital must be protected from mass democracy, from citizens wanting to place limits on the global flow of capital. Contrary to common understanding, the mindset does not simply oppose states and markets, it does not say that markets must be liberated from the state; rather, it says that markets must be protected from democracy, and states must first formulate international rules (such as through the WTO, the IMF and World Bank) which ensure the freedom of capital, and then enforce those rules within their own territory, whatever the preferences of their citizens. That coercive function is the primary economic function of the state. The EU, with its sacred four freedoms of capital, goods, services and labour, represents a triumph of this mindset (Slobodian 2018).

Notice that the resulting public policy prescriptions have no place for the value of community, social connections, common purpose, or identification with place (no place for 'somewhere' people as distinct from 'anywhere' people, in David Goodhart's distinction). Implicitly, they sanction egotistical go-getting as the modus operandi of the good society. Like it or not, the conservative doctrine constitutes a coherent moral vision based on the premise that the 'market' is natural and should be expanded and the 'state' is artificial and should be limited. It is more coherent than anything the social democratic or centre-left moral vision has produced.

'Fiscal responsibility', coupled with the state narrowly but actively protecting property rights and free capital mobility, have won acceptance among politicians, policymakers and economists because the mindset benefits the asset-rich and those enjoying income from owning and managing capital (mostly privately-concerned 'anywhere' people). The capitalist classes lobby governments directly to institutionalise these conservative norms, and indirectly shape the intellectual understanding of what constitutes serious policy. Serious policy says, 'lower public borrowing brings lower borrowing costs for the private sector, lower public spending brings more scope for private profit-seeking, lower taxes bring higher profits'. Then the visceral appeal of 'tax-as-theft', and 'a rising tide lifts all boats', reaches through to enough voters to put anything more than modest social democracy and downward income redistribution beyond the reach of governments in most western democracies, except to curb extreme poverty.

The outcome of public policy skewed to the interests of the wealthy has been a spectacular sluicing up of income to the top of the distribution, especially in the USA. Here are a pair of figures which illustrate how American society became so bitterly polarised. First, the real income of the richest one percent galloped ahead at the average rate of 2.6 percent a year over the 38 years from 1979 to 2017. Second, taking the middle class as the 20th to the 80th percentile of the income distribution, average income of the US middle class grew at the barely perceptible rate of 1.3 percent a year over the same period; and probably grew *backwards* when one adds in healthcare and education, whose costs have grown significantly faster than the consumer price index. Another pair of figures makes basically the same point. Fifty years ago, in 1970, a typical US CEO of a listed firm earned about 20 times as much as the typical worker. Today, thanks to 'globalisation', and to the linked radical changes to procedures for setting management pay and bonuses made in the 1990s, the CEO earns about 350 times as much.

But right up to a decade ago, the rise of income concentration was a non-problem for economists and most western countries' policymakers. Margaret Thatcher gave the standard rejection in her 1990 slap-down of a Labour member of Parliament expressing worries about income inequality: 'The honourable member is saying that he would rather that the poor were poorer, provided the rich were less rich.... What a policy!' In 2007, London School of Economics professor of economics Willem Buiter said in the *Financial Times*, 'Poverty bothers me. Inequality does not. I just don't care.'

The doctrine of 'fiscal responsibility' justified decades of neglect of public services across much of the western world, including local government services like public transport, libraries, youth centres, free school meals, swimming pools, and in some countries more than others, scandalous under-investment in physical infrastructure (notably the USA). The care-home industry was given over to private profit-seeking enterprises, with a built-in incentive to lower standards of care and underpay staff. The health insurance industry was given over to profit-seeking enterprises, with a built-in incentive to minimise people with pre-existing conditions and minimise out-payments.

Populist leaders, defined by their claim to speak for 'the real people' or 'the silent majority' and who treat opponents as enemies, have swept to power in democracies by appropriating and exploiting the feelings of helplessness, loneliness and resentment among the disadvantaged stoked up by these 'fiscal responsibility' policies. They offer followers a story of good and evil and the sense of personal meaning that comes from fighting a holy war. (Almost 90 percent of Trump voters, post election, believe the result is illegitimate, feeding the narrative of betrayal and injustice; and almost 90 percent say the Biden presidency will do 'lasting harm to the US'.) In this way the leaders direct mass attention from income concentration, precarious jobs, and cuts in public services, and focus it on the existence of Others or Thems living in the society (or trying to get in), who take power and resources from real people and the silent majority. Former President Obama relates in his *A promised land* that a Republican senator told him, 'I hate to say it, but the worse people feel right now, the better it is for us'. He may have hated to say it, but he loved to see it.

But this alone is not enough to give electoral majorities. Populist leaders combine it with attracting support and finance from the conservative financial and business establishments, whose members hold their noses and ignore smelly aspects of the personality and administration in exchange for property right enforcement, tax cuts, deregulation and opportunities for oligarchic enrichment, under the moral banner of 'fiscal responsibility'.

The received conservative truths about fiscal responsibility and limited state took a hammering after the North Atlantic Financial Crisis of 2008, when governments, led by the G20, launched internationally coordinated public spending programmes to offset the collapse of private spending. But then came a ferocious restoration of 'fiscal responsibility' across the west, as in German finance minister Wolfgang Schäuble's declaration, 'austerity is the only cure for the eurozone' (2011).

The global Covid crisis has forced governments to incur public deficits to limit the collapse of private sector production and employment on a scale relative to gross domestic product (GDP) not seen since the second world war. It has turned the spotlight on the decrepit condition of many public infrastructures and services, the minimum pay of 'key' public sector workers, and vast income and education disparities. But what happens once the Covid crisis is dealt with? A repeat of 2008 and the hard swing back to deregulation and cuts in public services under the banner of 'fiscal responsibility'?

Opening economists' minds
This time we do see momentum for lasting change in mindset, coming from several quarters. For one, the pressure on governments to run the biggest public deficits since the second world war has brought the heterodox doctrine called modern monetary theory (MMT) in from the far margins to give some (contested) assurance that a government with a sovereign currency can safely sustain much higher levels of public debt, provided inflation remains low. MMT contributes to win a broader rejection of the ur-metaphor that gave the conservative doctrine much of its emotional appeal to the mammalian part of our brain: the government is like a household writ large, and as a household must cut its spending when its income falls, so must a government (the metaphorical logic behind 'austerity is the only cure for the eurozone').

Also, research findings that had previously been confined to the margins command more respect. In the past few years, and more emphatically in 2020, IMF researchers have published findings that run against decades of IMF doctrine: fiscal stimulus can be effective; capital controls can be a valuable tool of macroeconomic management; raising public investment by 1 percent of GDP typically raises private investment by much more than 1 percent; and measures to lower income inequality typically bring growth gains greater than the losses caused by the measures to make the redistribution (IMF 2020, Sandbu 2020). The IMF's *imprimateur* makes it easier for national governments to adopt policy norms beyond the Washington consensus.

Foreword

Even 'industrial policy' no longer provokes a knee-jerk rejection – as in 'governments can't pick winners' and 'the best industrial policy is none at all', mind-numbing slogans echoed in ministries of finance and economics around the capitalist world (Wade 2016, 2017, Cherif *et al.* 2020). The pandemic has highlighted what was in plain sight but mostly unseen – capitalism can work well when the government exercises its power to guide the market economy, impart 'directional thrust', and act as the ultimate absorber of risk for investors and for citizens at large. In particular, the state has to undertake or induce private sector entities to undertake pre-commercial research in biology, chemistry, physics, maths and AI for which there is not sufficient profit incentive – provided that the state has a risk-reward contract to receive a share of the later commercial profits, as would a venture capitalist. All the time, the state-market dilemma must be safely navigated: business needs the state and the state needs business; but business can corrupt the state, the state can corrupt business (Wade 1995).

The Covid opening for new economic thinking joins up with the older opening made by global warming. The latter has crystallised fundamental issues like 'is green growth possible?'. Those discussions inevitably raise the question of growth itself, how we measure it, how we should measure it. Ever since the Kennedy government's Commerce Department in 1961 stuck signs on every wall, 'What have you done for growth today?' – the first time in history that GDP growth had been taken as the number one (economic) objective of a government – we have rejoiced when growth rises by percentage points and lamented when it falls by percentage points (notwithstanding that a few years later John Kennedy's brother Robert liked to say during his 1968 presidential campaign that GDP measures everything 'except that which makes life worthwhile').

Thinking about global warming cannot avoid the distinction between good growth and bad growth. Bad growth includes that component of GDP growth attributable to fossil-fuel subsidies, whose harmful effects (including on global warming) should be subtracted from growth; likewise for expenditures on clearing up the environmental costs 'externalised' by private agents polluting rivers and cutting forests. We might even include in bad growth the increment gained by following *New York Times* journalist Thomas Friedman's tongue-in-cheek suggestion that – thanks to Trump culture making lying into a growth industry – we include the 'lying sector' with its own GDP line, alongside clothing, autos, and financial services (Friedman 2020).

Still another source of new economic thinking is the spreading worry about the previous 'non-problem' of income inequality. One indicator is the astonishing sales (hardback and ebook) of Thomas Piketty's *Capital* – a clunky, 600 plus page book about income and wealth inequality: in the first year after publication of the English translation, 2014–2015, about 1.5 million copies globally – though according to a crude Amazon measure, the average Kindle reader stopped on page 12, smashing the previous record for least pages read long held by Steven Hawking's *A brief history of time*, whose average Kindle reader stopped on page 16 (Wade 2014).

Heather Boushey, at the Washington Center for Equitable Growth, explained, 'As someone who advises policy-makers, I can tell you there is often this shock: "The economy is growing. Why aren't people feeling it?" The answer is: because they literally aren't feeling it.' (Leonhardt 2018). A woman at a 'Remain' rally in the north of England (a rally to secure support for Britain remaining in the European Union in the coming referendum of 2016) expressed the same point, more succinctly. The speaker

| Foreword

was describing the terrible hit to GDP of Britain's exit. The woman shouted out, 'That's your GDP, not ours!' Polling evidence suggests that large swathes of the public think that talk about 'the economy' is talk about some entity unrelated to their own lives and employment and wellbeing, it is something related to elites and people who talk like robots (Wade 2020).

The evident real-world unhappiness has filtered through to some economists who have begun to focus attention on professional economic ethics. Economics has been an ethics-free zone, much freer than any of the other social sciences, a legacy of neoclassical economics' embrace of late nineteenth century physics as its model. But 2016 saw the publication of *The Oxford handbook of professional economic ethics*, edited by George DeMartino and Deirdre McCloskey, which you might think is a slender pocketbook but in fact is even fatter and heavier than Piketty's *Capital*.

The sense that free-market capitalism is not delivering is captured in the trend of responses to questions about satisfaction or dissatisfaction with democracy. The rise in dissatisfaction in the English-speaking democracies since around 2005, led by the USA, is striking. And across 77 democracies, with combined population of 2.4 bn, the percentage of respondents expressing dissatisfaction with democracy has exceeded 50 percent in almost every year since 2008 (Wolf 2020). We live in a global democratic recession.

The evidence of multiplying discontent has given rise to the linked fields of happiness and wellbeing studies. Their central paradox is that rising prosperity (measured by GDP) has typically, at least in high income countries, been accompanied by rising unhappiness and mental illness rather than the reverse – for example, a rising proportion of people who say they are not pleased with how their life has progressed. In response, the past two decades have seen an upsurge of attention to societal happiness and how to raise it – for example economist Richard Layard's *Happiness: lessons from a new science* (2005) and psychologist Oliver James's *Affluenza* (2007).

But societal happiness as an objective of economic policy has a much older history. Sociologist Richard Titmuss during the second world war found, to general surprise, that the war coincided with improved mental health. He attributed this not only to the cohesive effect of facing a common enemy but also to the impact of universal services which became available during the war, from free school meals to pensions. These created what Titmuss described as 'less social disparities', which led to better morale and mental health.

Another important contribution came from Tibor Scitovsky and *The joyless economy* in 1976, which engaged directly with the paradox that higher incomes do not produce higher happiness, suggesting we should measure the latter directly, because of the wisdom in the saying 'we treasure what we measure'. The psychologist Martin Seligman popularised the term 'wellbeing' in the early 2000s and promoted the 'positive psychology' movement for teaching happiness in schools.

The opening to wellbeing as real (not just rhetorical) national objective

Looking on the bright side, the combination of global warming, soaring income concentration, falling levels of happiness, democracy in recession, and now the Covid pandemic might be enough to keep policymakers' and economists' minds more open than in the wake of the 2008 crash even after Covid is back in the bottle, more willing to engage with new approaches to previously neglected objectives, less zealous to return to fiscal responsibility, market discipline, bowling alone and egotistical go-getting as the spine of a moral society. This is the context in which to appreciate Girol Karacaoglu's new book on the design and implementation of public policy to promote not just wellbeing but intergenerational wellbeing 'as if it mattered'. [1]

The book's direction of travel is given in this statement:

> There is now an emerging consensus on the need to augment income with complementary measures of wellbeing in evaluating the success of public policy, since income is not a good proxy for all indicators of wellbeing.

It elaborates the moral frame that supports the expansion from growth of conventionally measured GDP as our most important objective to a multidimensional index of wellbeing, including income as one dimension. And it proceeds to spell out how a government, with New Zealand specifics, could make this switch.

New Zealand has already won plaudits internationally for injecting wellbeing as an important objective of government policy across the board. Treasury officials travelled the world (pre-Covid) describing the process to appreciative audiences. But one has to be vigilant against the wellbeing equivalent of 'greenwashing' or 'ESG washing' (environmental, social, corporate governance). When a firm advertises its environmental concern and puts the work in the hands of the marketing director rather than the CEO or equivalent, you can be fairly sure it is greenwashing. Similarly when a department of government, or the government as a whole, declares its commitment to wellbeing as its chief objective, not GDP growth as such, we have to ask, how much is

---

[1] *Love you* joins books about 'governing the future' by another member of the same School of Government at Victoria University of Wellington of which Girol is the current Head of School – namely, Jonathan Boston's *Future-proofing the state* (ANU Press, 2014), *Safeguarding the future* (BWB, 2017) and *Governing for the future* (Emerald, 2017).

'wellbeing washing' a gloss on a website?

What we citizens want to know – this would need another book – is how much difference the introduction of wellbeing objectives has made to the advice of officials in Treasury and other departments over resource allocation ('taxpayers' money'), at the top of hierarchies and near the bottom, at 'street level'. We would also like to know what are the targets (not just feel-good words) for reducing income concentration, as a step towards higher wellbeing in society at large. For example, the richest 20 percent in Scandinavia have an average income some 3.5 to 4 times that of the average of the bottom 20 percent. The figure for the USA and UK is 7 to 8 times. New Zealand is 5.6. What could and should be done to bring the New Zealand figure down to, say, 5.0 or even 4.5? Would the costs of doing so outweigh the benefits?

We would also like to know the steps being taken to strengthen New Zealand's generally weak local governments, in line with the localisation principles Girol elaborates (which at a general level were endorsed remarkably early in the Municipal Corporations Act 1842, as quoted here); steps which should include citizens' assemblies with recommending authority. Such localisation might strengthen *positive* feedback of the wellbeing approach, as against the *negative* feedback sure to come from many of the asset-rich and those enjoying income from owning and managing capital, not to mention many mainstream economists. The issue of how to institutionalise positive feedback is critical for the sustainability of the wellbeing approach – because its sustainability runs smack into the collective action problem, that the benefits are widely diffused while many of the costs are concentrated on unappreciative asset-owners.

Put another way, the issue is how to create mechanisms, including citizen assemblies, that keep the state operating as a caring and guiding state, without damaging private enterprise, rather than operating as the grabbing hand of oligarchic elites using wellbeing as a mask for private economic and political gain.

Yes, 'fiscal responsibility' is code for a moral order that privileges status over fairness; but 'fiscal irresponsibility' can be even worse — see Argentina and Weimer Republic, most of whose citizens longed for a good dose of 'responsibility'. Yes, modern monetary theory usefully expands the legitimate scope of public spending; but only where people have confidence in the government's capacity to run a balanced budget and in the central bank's discipline not to engage in a printing festival, even as it speaks favourably of MMT. Yes, more government involvement in national resource allocation is needed – active labour market policies, public investment bank, R&D policy, wage subsidies, affordable housing, libraries, free museums, subsidies to farmers and grocers to offer affordable fruit and vegetables in low-income areas; but there is a thin line between guided capitalism and crony-capitalism, as seen in America where it is often more profitable to invest in lobbying than in R&D. The problem is that these complexities break the binary moral narrative of good and bad, and hence do not appeal to many voters, politicians and mainstream economists. Post Covid, we will see high tension between those demanding 're-globalisation' and a big retrenchment in government spending (forgetting that 'fiscal austerity' was a main reason why a resilient recovery failed to emerge after 2010), and those pressing to rethink national objectives and the role of government.

Girol's is an important addition to this debate. He steers the narrative between the complexities as beautifully and tightly woven as a Turkish carpet. Along the way he presents gems like these words from Antoine de Saint-Exupery, 'If you want to build a ship, don't drum up people to collect wood and don't assign them tasks and work, but rather teach them to long for the endless immensity of the sea'. The same for reorienting public policy towards wellbeing.

Robert H. Wade is professor of global political economy at the London School of Economics. Son of a New Zealand diplomat, educated at Wellington College, Otago University, Victoria University, and Sussex University, he has worked at the Institute of Development Studies (Sussex University), the World Bank, Princeton University, MIT, and Brown University; and done field work in Pitcairn Island, Italy, India, South Korea, Taiwan and inside the World Bank. His book *Governing the market* (1990, 2004) won the American Political Science Association's Best Book or Article in Political Economy, 1989–1991. He was awarded the Leontief Prize in Economics in 2008.

References
Cherif, Reda, Marc Engher and Fuad Hasanov (2020), 'Crouching beliefs, hidden biases: the rise and fall of growth narratives', IMF Working Papers, 8 November (Washington: International Monetary Fund).
DeMartino, George and Deidre McCloskey (eds) (2016), *The Oxford handbook of Professional Economics Ethics* (Oxford: Oxford University Press).
Friedman, Thomas (2020), 'Only truth can save America', *New York Times (International)*, 12 November.
Goodhart, David (2017), *The road to somewhere: the new tribes shaping British politics* (Harmondsworth: Penguin).
IMF (2020), *World economic outlook* (Washington: International Monetary Fund).
James, Oliver (2007), *Affluenza* (London: Vermillion).
Layard, Richard (2005), *Happiness: lessons from a new science* (Harmondsworth: Allen Lane).

Leonhardt, David (2018), 'We're measuring the economy all wrong', *New York Times* (International), 15–16 September.

Pistor, Katherina (2019), *The code of capital: how the law creates wealth and inequality* (Princeton: Princeton University Press).

Sandbu, Martin (2020), 'Dawn breaks on a new era of thinking', *Financial Times*, 12 October.

Schäuble, Wolfgang (2011), 'Why austerity is only cure for the eurozone', *Financial Times*, 5 September.

Slobodian, Quinn (2018), *Globalists: the end of empire and the birth of neoliberalism* (Boston: Harvard University Press).

Wade, Robert H. (1995), 'Resolving the state-market dilemma in East Asia', in *The role of the state in economic change*, (eds.) Ha-Joon. Chang and Robert Rowthorn (Oxford: Clarendon Press).

Wade, Robert H. (2014), 'The Piketty phenomenon and the future of inequality', *Real-world economics review*, 69, special issue on Piketty's Capital.

Wade, Robert H. (2016), Industrial policy in response to the middle-income trap and the third wave of the digital revolution', *Global policy*, November, http://onlinelibrary.wiley.com/doi/10.1111/gpol.2016.7.issue-4/issuetoc.

Wade, Robert H. (2017), 'The America paradox: ideology of free markets and hidden practice of directional thrust', *Cambridge journal of economics* 41 (3), May.

Wade, Robert H. (2020) 'Globalisation, inequality and poverty: power and evidence in "best practice" economic policy', chapter 12, John Ravenhill (ed), *Global political economy*, 6th edition (Oxford: Oxford University Press).

Wolf, Martin (2020) 'Democracy in a time of division', *Financial Times*, 11 November.

 Preface

In *The faith of a heretic* (1961), the German philosopher Walter Kaufman proposes four cardinal virtues as a foundation for answering the following questions: How are we to live? By what standards should we judge ourselves? For what virtues should we strive? His four cardinal virtues are: 'humbition' (a made-up word referring to a fusion of humility and ambition), love, courage, and honesty.

It is the second one of these (love) that is the centre of interest for this book. Kaufman gives the word a very specific meaning. As Wes Cecil, the producer and narrator of the lecture series *Forgotten thinkers*, interprets it, 'I love you' for Kaufman means:

> 'I desire for you the same way that I desire for me – I want you to have what you want, what you wish, what you need, and to avoid what you do not want, exactly the same way I feel about it for me. Not that I want the same things for you as I do for me; but if you think you want something, I have the desire for you to get it as strongly as you do.'

In short, 'I love you' means that I want you to live the life that you want to live. I will be as happy as you, if you do; and as unhappy as you, if you don't.

This book asks and answers the question: how would we design, govern, implement, and evaluate public policy if we based it on our love for future generations, true to the meaning that Kaufman gives to: 'I love you'?

We have no idea what future generations will value and how they will want to live. Nor do we wish to prescribe how they should choose to live – so long as they don't prevent others from living the lives they value. We want to prepare and look after the 'wellbeing garden' (the broader ecosystems) that will provide them with the opportunities and capabilities to *survive* and *thrive* – to flourish in safety. As Walter Benjamin expressed it, 'We want to liberate the future from its deformation in the present'.[2]

Wellbeing is about the ability of individuals and communities to live the lives they value – now and in the future – as an aspect of their human rights.[3] To prevent the enjoyment of valued lives would frustrate those rights. Ensuring justice across generations should guide a public policy that has intergenerational wellbeing as its objective.

This book covers the processes by which wellbeing-focused public policy objectives should be established, prioritised, implemented, managed along the way, funded, and evaluated on an ongoing basis – while also ensuring that they remain relevant as social preferences change over time. In short, it is about governing and investing for intergenerational wellbeing.

---

[2] Wellmon (2020).
[3] See Hunt (2007) on the evolution of human rights as an idea.

1. Introduction

Bache and Reardon (2016) suggest that the (re)emergence of *wellbeing* as an explicit policy objective over the last ten years or so, with the term *wellbeing* highlighted, reflects a confluence of several developments. There is the growing realisation that the more recent (say over the last thirty years) primary focus of public policy on material sources of wellbeing (economic growth and so on) is not delivering the other sources that people care about. In fact, these other sources of wellbeing (such as environmental quality, social connections, and the absence of poverty in the sense of deprivation) are deteriorating.

This is becoming a global trend, one that is very visible thanks to the increasing availability of relevant data. Reflecting growing popular discontent and public pressure, there is a strengthening political will, supported by such data, financial resources, and analytical capability, to do something about it. The term *wellbeing policy* has emerged as a slogan, or umbrella term, for all these activities.

The opening remarks of the OECD Secretary-General Angel Gurria to the OECD international workshop on *Putting wellbeing metrics into policy action* (2–4 October 2019), as well as all the presentations at that workshop, provide strong confirmation and plenty of evidence in support of these claims.

Gurria refers to concerning challenges relating to poverty

and related vulnerabilities, widening economic inequalities (now also affecting the middles classes), rising unemployment and labour-market insecurities (especially affecting the young), persistent gender divides on pay and other market outcomes, falling average life satisfaction, rising mental disorders, fewer people reporting that they have friends and family to count on in times of need, diminishing voice and influence on what governments do, and increasing concerns about climate change and biodiversity.

He concludes by urging governments to rethink their policy priorities, balancing the recent focus on sustaining economic growth with people-focused policies that promote wellbeing and sustainable development. There is a need for an urgent transition from measurement to action, to address these issues.

The failure of public policy to deliver better lives for everyone, and therefore the need for a radically different approach to public policy and public management, constitutes the springboard for this book. 'A key empirically-based argument ... is the point that, since the Second World War in particular, governments have introduced a range of policies in domains closely associated with wellbeing (for example in education, health, and social welfare) without a discernible impact on aggregate levels of – specifically – happiness'.[4]

As the contributions from several countries to the OECD workshop referred to earlier highlighted, there is a strong will to address these concerns, and plenty of resources are available to do so. There is little evidence to give us confidence, however, that we possess the knowhow to convert these into wellbeing outcomes. We find ourselves searching for our lost keys under the wrong street light, using frameworks, concepts, and tools not suited to address the problems at hand.

---

[4] Bache and Reardon (2016), p133.

Introduction

Table 1 (extracted from the *Wellbeing Budget 2019*) shows the New Zealand record of this failure. This is not the New Zealand we want our grandchildren to inherit. We correctly label the problems highlighted in Table 1 as 'wicked problems' but seem to have no idea how we should tackle them. To use the language of Kay and King (2020), they present major risks to our 'reference narratives' – our core values and long-established way of life as a society.

We now have multiple definitions of happiness or wellbeing, several academic disciplines bringing a variety of perspectives to these concepts, lots of survey-based evidence to identify the sources of wellbeing, numerous indicators for each of these 'domains of wellbeing', a multiplicity of measures for each of these indicators, reliable estimates of correlations between them, methods to do cost-benefit analyses using 'wellbeing' (rather than dollars) as the 'currency' for such analyses, and much more.[5]

But we seem to be at a loss regarding how to improve wellbeing – both the key contributors to wellbeing (such as mental health), and wellbeing generally. The purpose of this book is to suggest a way of closing this gap and equipping public policy to work towards improving wellbeing.

Policy refers to a deliberate effort to influence the outcomes of activities ('deliberative choice of a calculative kind'[6]) organised by businesses, communities, non-government organisations, governments, and other entities. It includes the design, implementation, and evaluation of such efforts, as well as planning for responses to failures.

In the case of *public* policy, which is all about making choices on behalf of society at large (i.e. social or collective choices),

---
[5] Adler and Fleurbaey 2016; Frijters *et al.* (2019).
[6] Williamson (2000), p597.

Table 1. Examples of evidence behind the wellbeing budget priorities

Taking mental health seriously	Improving child wellbeing	Supporting Māori and Pasifika aspirations	Building a productive nation	Transforming the economy
Mental health In any year, one in five New Zealanders will have a diagnosable mental illness, with three-quarters of lifetime cases starting by the age of 25	**Material hardship** Around 150,000 children in New Zealand live in households experiencing material hardship	**Living standards** Māori and Pacific people rank low in most measures of wellbeing relative to the rest of the population	**R&D expenditure** New Zealand has low research and development (R&D) expenditure relative to OECD countries	**Greenhouse gas emissions** New Zealand has one of the highest per capita rates of greenhouse gas emissions in the OECD
Suicide rates New Zealand's suicide rate for young people is among the worst in the OECD	**Health outcomes** 41,000 children are hospitalised each year for conditions associated with deprivation	**Income level disparities** Māori and Pacific people have lower income levels, on average, than other groups	**Future of work and automation** 21 percent of current workforce tasks may be automated by 2030	**Quality of waterways** Waterways in our farming areas have markedly higher pollution than in catchments dominated by native vegetation
Homelessness One in 100 New Zealanders are homeless, based on the 2013 Census	**Family violence** New Zealand has high rates of family violence	**Educational attainment** Māori and Pacific people are less likely to attain higher educational qualifications than other groups	**Productivity** New Zealand's productivity is lower relative to other OECD countries	**Soil erosion** Annual soil erosion of 720 tonnes per square kilometre is reducing our land's productivity and harming aquatic ecosystems
Young people in employment 12 percent of young people aged 15–24 years are not in education, employment or training	**Crowded housing** Over 40 percent of Pacific children and roughly 25 percent of Māori children live in crowded homes	**Disparities in health status** Māori and Pacific people are less likely to report good, very good or excellent health than other groups	**Incomes** New Zealand's incomes are in the bottom half of the OECD as measured by per capita Gross Domestic Product (GDP)	**Waste** New Zealand's level of waste per capita has increased substantially since 2013

Source: New Zealand Government (2019).

Introduction

the effort is organised and managed by government, through its various agencies and departments. In this context 'the government' is the generic term we use to refer to any collective agency (central, regional, and/or local) through which we may wish to organise the production and/or delivery of 'public goods' – goods or services whose production or consumption benefit or hurt a wider group of people than the direct producers and consumers of these goods and services.

Public policy can be thought of as the bridge between private actions and broader environmental, social, and economic outcomes. As individuals and communities try to improve their lives, some of their actions have wider benefits such as the creation of beautiful music or scientific breakthroughs (positive *externalities*, in economists' language) but they may also incur broader costs, such as pollution or epidemics (negative *externalities*). We could think of the main purpose of public policy as furnishing the preconditions for human flourishing by magnifying actions that have wider social and environmental benefits, while minimising actions that have wider costs.

Public policy has multiple layers. This book delves into the design and implementation of public policy at a *system level* as it relates to the 'large world'.[7] It explores and provides an answer to the questions, how do we create the natural, social, and economic environment (*opportunities*) where the pursuit of valued lives is possible, and fashion the acquisition of the *capabilities* that enable the pursuit of these valued lives?

Why public policy?

Individuals and communities are constantly striving to live the lives they value, subject to their capabilities and opportunities,

---

[7] As Kay and King (2020) refer to it.

and conditioned by the constraints they encounter. They do so in a social setting. The natural question that then arises is, why is it the business of government to support their endeavours?

Factors well beyond the control of individuals and communities will significantly constrain their striving for wellbeing. Examples of such factors include environmental quality; the infrastructure required to support economic activity (such as roads, railways and broadband); the institutions (courts, parliament and democratic elections) that ensure personal freedoms and political voice; and social cohesion. These all have some features of 'public goods' – sources of wider benefits ('positive externalities') that enrich individual and social life on a sustained basis.

Individuals and communities (especially smaller ones) would have neither the incentives nor the resources to invest adequately in these public goods, although they would benefit hugely from having access to them.

I'm not suggesting here that the benefits associated with these positive externalities would not be provided at all in the absence of government action. But they may be under-provided. It is likely that 'decentralised market decisions lead to the under-provision of public goods such as infrastructure, or the over-provision of public bads such as pollution' (Sachs 2015, p155). Through appropriate and deliberate collective action, we may be able to make markets, communities, and institutions work more effectively and efficiently in delivering these public goods.[8]

Of course, public policy does not need to be grounded exclusively in such notions of 'market failure'. Mazzucato (2016) for one emphasises the wider role of public policy in the economic domain (going beyond simply fixing market and/or system fail-

---

[8] Haldane (2015).

ures), by drawing on a vast literature on the subject. She, like Tirole (2017), highlights the complementary roles of the state and markets; Rajan (2019) adds another pillar – communities. Mazzucato argues that when governed effectively and efficiently, 'the State's visible hand is firm but not heavy, providing the vision and the dynamic push (as well as some "nudges") to make things happen that otherwise would not have'.[9]

In any case, as Schmidt (2015) argues, referring to the 'fallacy of failure thinking', the debate about 'market failure' versus 'government failure' as it relates to the common good, is a logically and empirically unresolvable ideological debate. From this perspective, the search for optimal policies based on an equilibrium framework is a meaningless and futile exercise. In a world of 'radical uncertainty' and 'adaptive complexity',[10] there is no exogenously given 'optimum' (equilibrium) benchmark against which we can assess the performance of markets, the government, or any other set of institutions; so 'failure' cannot be determined.

Markets, governments and communities are all imperfect institutions, whatever that may mean. The key is to acknowledge this, as well as the complementary strengths of all these entities towards improving overall wellbeing, when they do function reasonably well. We should design public policy in a way that enhances the governance of all these institutions, with the aim of enhancing their collective efficiency and effectiveness in improving individual and community wellbeing.

Finally, economics, as a discipline, does not have a monopoly on framing and evaluating public policy. As I will argue, the wicked problems we are facing around the world require a multidisciplinary approach. There are all kinds of reasons in addition

---

[9] Mazzucato, 2015, p2.
[10] See chapter 2 in this book.

to economic ones, including moral and ethical, for which governments may choose to influence individual and community decisions and actions – again because they want to magnify the good and minimise the wrong or the harmful from a broader social and environmental perspective.

Philosophical and ethical foundations

One cannot develop public policy recommendations in an ethical and philosophical void.[11] Following Sen (1999, 2009) I take the view that wellbeing is all about human beings and the communities to which they belong having the capabilities and opportunities (i.e. substantial freedoms) to live the kinds of lives they value, and have reason to value.[12]

The philosophical and ethical foundations on which the policy framework of this book are built are well summarised by Layard and O'Donnell (2015). After quoting Thomas Jefferson ('The care of human life and happiness [...] is the only legitimate object of good government'), they write: 'What should be the goal of public policy? We agree with Thomas Jefferson. What matters is the quality of life, as people themselves experience it. And the best judge of each person's life is that same person. Is she happy with her life; is she satisfied? In a democracy that should be the criterion for good policy.'[13]

As the United States Declaration of Independence (1776) expressed it, 'We hold these truths to be self-evident, that all men are created equal, that they are endowed by their Creator with certain unalienable Rights, that among these are Life, Liberty and *the pursuit of Happiness* [my emphasis].'[14]

---

[11] Sen (2009).
[12] See Karacaoglu, King, and Krawczyk (2019), and Reid (2019) for an extensive list of references.
[13] Ibid., p77.
[14] The emphasis is mine.

Introduction

Providing the 'enablers' (in the form of improved capabilities and opportunities) to achieve a better life is simply a necessary condition; it does not guarantee the achievement of better outcomes, a better life. Indeed, 'the key idea behind the capabilities approach is that individuals differ in their ability to transform resources into wellbeing or "flourishing".'[15]

Undoubtedly, there are individuals (including young children) who, for all sorts of reasons, are not capable of being the best judges of their own wellbeing. Under such circumstances, the families, other loved ones and immediate communities surrounding them, are best placed to make these decisions for them.

If, to take an example, despite best efforts in the formulation and implementation of public policy, youth suicide keeps increasing in communities around the country, should this be a concern for public policy as well? Our answer is an emphatic 'yes'. The design and implementation of public policy need to be accountable for delivering a good life to all citizens, as individual citizens themselves wish to live it.

The rest of the book is structured as follows.

In chapter 2, I define wellbeing in terms of the ability of individuals and communities to live the lives they value, provided they do not interfere with others' rights to do the same. I provide six critical and complementary justifications for a radically different approach to public policy when its objective is to enhance wellbeing. First, wellbeing is *multidimensional*. Second, wellbeing is *intergenerational*. Third, the various dimensions and sources of wellbeing are strongly *interdependent*. Fourth, individual lives are lived in *social settings*. Fifth, the 'large world' in which our

---

[15] Chakravarty and Lugo (2016), p246.

social life is embedded is *radically* (or fundamentally) *uncertain*. Sixth, both individual and social lives are dominated by *adaptive complexity* and *reflexivity*. It is the universal and simultaneous presence of all six justifications that demand a radically different approach to public policy.

Chapter 3 articulates a framework for a wellbeing-focused public policy in a world of radical or fundamental uncertainty and complexity. At a *system* level, such a framework has three complementary dimensions. First, an environment (natural, social, and economic environment – the 'wellbeing garden') which makes the pursuit of valued lives possible (i.e. the *opportunities*). Second, investments that provide individuals and communities with the *capabilities* to pursue their valued lives. Third, a shift of policy focus from *direction* to *nourishment* – from looking for 'optimal solutions' to well-defined problems, to *building resilience* to potential (unknown) systemic risks that threaten valued ways of living, partly by encouraging creative responses to systemic shocks through both individual initiative and cooperative community mechanisms.

Chapter 4 further develops the theme that in a world of fundamental uncertainty, *investing in resilience* provides the critical bridge to the sustainability of wellbeing across generations. Wellbeing-resilience has two key and complementary dimensions: *surviving* and *thriving*. These will be delivered through investments that create the capacities to absorb systemic shocks to how we want to live (*surviving*), as well as adapt towards enhancing our collective wellbeing in the aftermath of shocks (*thriving*). In an intergenerational context, adaptability also involves the ability to respond positively to the changing preferences of younger generations. The chapter also discusses ways in which resilience to potential systemic risks can be built.

Chapter 5 is about governance arrangements underpinning

Introduction

a wellbeing-focused public policy. I argue that, in a world dominated by radical (or fundamental) uncertainty and adaptive complexity, a public policy that aspires to deliver sustainable wellbeing across generations as its primary *outcome*, needs to be supported by governance arrangements that can deliver five critical *outputs*: a long-term focus on policy making; inclusive decision-making mechanisms that aggregate the wisdom, expertise and experience of all stakeholders; institutions that enable and encourage (and indeed mandate) an integrated environmental, social and economic approach to public policy; a suitable supporting funding infrastructure; and adaptive time consistency, that is ongoing alignment of public policy with collective wellbeing as the preferences of society evolve over time.

Chapter 6 places communities at the centre of inclusive policy processes, and explores different avenues for giving effect to inclusivity. Individual and family lives are lived in social settings, and the imperative of social cohesion for sustainable wellbeing means that the engagement of communities as full participants in the end-to-end public policy and management process is critical. Amartya Sen (2018) refers to this as evidence-informed and discussion-based, participatory governance. In a world of adaptive complexity, in the absence of genuine community engagement and participation, it is impossible to generate sustainable improvements in social cohesion and environmental quality. I acknowledge however that *localism* does not provide a panacea; and ensuring genuine participation by communities is a major governance challenge in itself.

Chapter 7 is about the assessment of the effectiveness of a wellbeing-focused public policy. I argue that four complementary types of assessment are required. First, whether more resources are being made available to support better lives. Second, whether these resources are being converted into higher capabilities and opportunities for a better life. Third, asking people whether their lives are improving or not. Fourth, whether public policy is creating the platform in the form of a suitable wellbeing garden for sustainable intergenerational wellbeing.

Chapter 8 looks at policy priorities. I argue that, given where New Zealand is right now as a country, the top two priorities of a public policy that has intergenerational wellbeing as its primary objective should be a universal and comprehensive 'leave no one behind' strategy, complemented by long-term environment-friendly investments that generate sustained employment growth.

Chapter 9 highlights the congruence and alignment of individual and social wellbeing. It proposes that when individuals live lives that enhance collective wellbeing, their individual wellbeing also improves.

This book was substantially completed before the Covid-19 pandemic rolled across the world. While most unfortunate, this event nevertheless provides a perfect platform for rethinking public policy in a radically different way. In the epilogue, I take the opportunity to highlight how a wellbeing framework can be helpful in designing and implementing public policy in response to Covid-19 in a way that enhances wellbeing across generations.

I will be using the term *ecosystems* frequently throughout this book. I use this term in the sense of a community of interacting organisms and their natural, social, physical and economic environments. These organisms can be human beings and non-humans, as well as institutions (such as the government, courts of law, and banks). They may take the form of complex networks, or interconnected systems, and their effective and efficient func-

Wellbeing and a radically different policy approach

tioning is critical for, among other things, social cohesion, environmental health and financial stability.

One of the most critical messages of this book is that unless an integrated environmental, social, cultural and economic policy framework is adopted, taking into account the critical interdependencies between associated ecosystems, a public policy that is focused on intergenerational wellbeing cannot achieve its objectives. Human lives are lived in social settings, and society is embedded in a natural environment.

There are two other senses in which I advocate an *integrated* approach to public policy and public management. The first is *multi-disciplinarity*, drawing on political science, philosophy, history, sociology, psychology, biology, and economics to inform thinking about public policy. The second is a reference to *inclusivity* in the processes followed in designing and implementing public policy, drawing on the wisdom and experience of all those who will be affected by it, across different levels of government, the scientific and business communities, and NGOs, as well as different genders and ethnicities.

Finally, and critically, I question the usefulness of a public policy that is based exclusively on any particular ideology or school of thought. Very much in the spirit of Beinhocker's (2016) argument, I believe that the profound environmental, social and economic problems we are facing make the traditional left vs right debates irrelevant. We have a lot to learn from all schools of thought. My aim is to suggest an approach to public policy and management that reflects their collective wisdom, towards improving human lives now and into the future.

Love you – *Public policy for intergenerational wellbeing*

2. Wellbeing and a radically different policy approach

Our public policy platform is the concept of love introduced in the Preface. The objective of public policy is to make it possible for individuals and communities to live the kinds of lives they value, in the present and into the future without compromising others' rights to do the same. This is what individual and community wellbeing is all about.

It follows that the key question facing a public policy that has intergenerational wellbeing as its objective, and respects the rights of individuals and communities to live the lives they value, is the following: how do we create the environment in which the pursuit of valued lives is possible; and then support universal access to the capabilities and opportunities (in terms of the *substantial freedoms*) that enable the pursuit of these valued lives?[16]

By approach to policy, we are referring to the end-to-end process of deciding on the challenges and opportunities that public policy should be focusing on; governance arrangements; prioritisation of outcomes and policies; funding; implementation; evaluation along the way, on the basis of effectiveness, efficiency, and equity; and planning for the possibility of failure.

In this setting, there are six critical yet complementary justifications underpinning the call for a radically different approach to public policy. First, wellbeing is *multi-dimensional*. Second,

---
[16] See Sen (1999, 2009), Nussbaum (1999, 2000), and Rawls (1971).

wellbeing is *intergenerational*. Third, both the various dimensions and sources of wellbeing are strongly *interdependent*. Fourth, individual lives are lived in *social settings*. Fifth, the 'large world' in which our social life is imbedded is *radically* (or fundamentally) *uncertain*.[17] Sixth, both individual and social lives are dominated by *adaptive complexity* and *reflexivity*.[18] It is the universal and simultaneous presence of all six justifications that demand a radically different approach to public policy.

I want to very briefly anticipate the primary consequences of these justifications for the approach to public policy advocated in this book before they are explored in detail in the chapters that follow.

The *multidimensional* aspect of wellbeing affects both the framing of the objective of public policy and the assessment or evaluation of public policy. The focus on *intergenerational wellbeing* has a major influence on how the policy approach is governed and implementation is funded. *Interdependence* affects the nature of the modelling work – in other words the evidence base – that informs the prioritisation of both public policies and supporting investments. *Radical uncertainty* shifts the focus of public policy from searching for optimal solutions to investing towards building resilience. *Complexity, reflexivity,* and the emphasis on *social settings* all affect the implementation of public policy and the nature of effective policy interventions, with a critical focus on inclusivity and effective participation by all stakeholders, that is participatory governance.

Multidimensionality
Although we do not know, nor do we wish to pass judgement on,

---
[17] Kay and King (2020).
[18] Soros (2013), Arthur (2014).

how people want to live their lives, we have the benefit of numerous studies covering a large variety of countries and cultures across time to help us identify the main influences on individual wellbeing. In other words, based primarily on robust, survey based, empirical evidence, we have a broad sense of the common elements of what individuals value.[19] These are summarised in figure 1.[20]

The key dimensions of current wellbeing represented in the upper half of figure 1 can be classified under the categories *quality of life* (health, work-life balance, knowledge and skills, social connections, civic engagement, environment quality, safety,

Figure 1. The OECD wellbeing framework

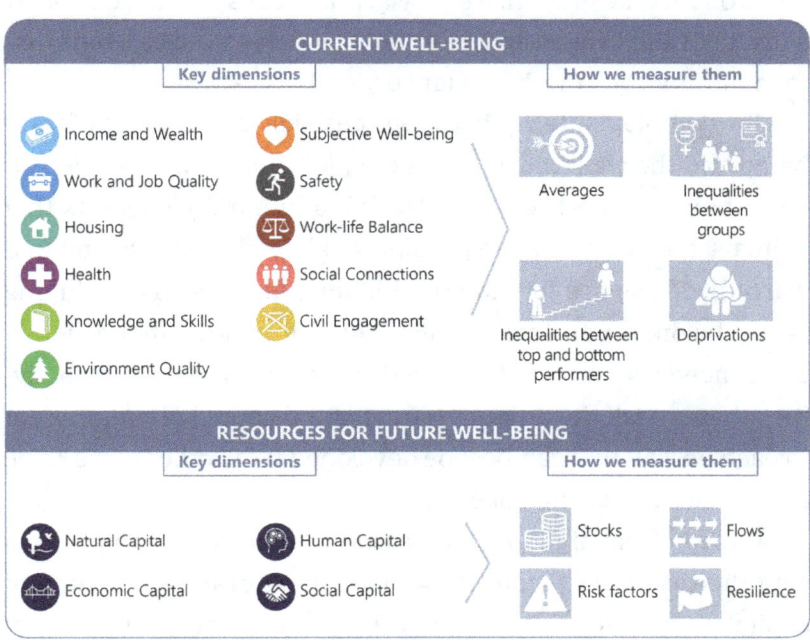

Source: OECD (2019 a).

---

[19] See Boarini *et al*. (2014), Smith (2015).
[20] See OECD (2020).

subjective wellbeing) and *material conditions* (income and wealth, work and job quality, housing). These can be conceptualised as primary goods, to use Rawls' term,[21] access to which is critical to achieving wellbeing in a broad sense.

The fundamental points highlighted by figure 1 and associated studies referred to above are as follows. Economic growth (income and other material sources of wellbeing) are necessary but not sufficient for wellbeing. In addition to their material comforts people care about many other aspects of life. Income can buy some of these other items (such as housing, education, …) but not all – for instance, social connections, civic engagement, good governance, clean environment. Furthermore, if we only focus on income growth, we may actually cause damage to other aspects of life that people care about, such as a clean environment (China), or work-life balance (South Korea).

The complementarity between these key dimensions of wellbeing and the well-known Maslow's hierarchy of needs[22] depicted in figure 2 is self-evident. Maslow's hierarchy suggests that primary human needs are physiological: food, water, shelter and warmth. These are followed by higher sets of needs, including safety, belonging and self-esteem. The highest level in the hierarchy of needs is described as self-actualisation and refers to activities that unlock the unique character and contribution inherent in each person that can best be developed if the other more basic needs are securely in place.

At the bottom of figure 1 are a set of capital stocks that represent the resources for future wellbeing: natural capital, human capital, social capital, and economic capital. Brief descriptions of these can be found in New Zealand Treasury (2019).

---

[21] Rawls (1971), pp90–95.
[22] Maslow (1943).

Wellbeing and a radically different policy approach

Figure 2.   Maslow's hierarchy of needs

Source: Highgate Counselling Centre,
http://highgatecounselling.org.uk/members/certificate/CT2%20Paper%201.pdf

In terms of these resources for future wellbeing, there are emerging concerns on a much wider front than simply material resources:

'Looking forward, there is no room for complacency. As storm clouds gather on the horizon, mainly from environmental and social challenges, all OECD countries need to take action if they are to maintain today's well-being for future generations.

'Nearly two-thirds of people in OECD countries are exposed to dangerous levels of air pollution. ... Reductions in greenhouse gas emissions (GHG) in the OECD are far from sufficient to meet climate policy goals and, in almost half of OECD countries, more species are at risk of extinction. Household debt in almost two-thirds of the OECD exceeds annual household disposable income and has deepened in a third of member states since 2010.

'While trust in government has improved by 3 percentage points on average since 2010, less than half of the population across OECD countries trust their institutions, and only 1 in 3 people feel they have a say in what the government does. Women hold just one-third of all seats in OECD parliaments, and hence, inclusive decision-making remains a distant goal.

'Overall, recent advances in well-being have not been matched by improvements in the resources needed to sustain well-being over time. From financial insecurity in households, through to climate change, biodiversity loss and threats to how democratic institutions perform their functions, we need to look beyond maximising well-being today. Ensuring continued prosperity for people and the planet will require bold and strategic investments in the resources that underpin well-being in the longer run.'[23]

Interdependence
There is a very large and rich literature on the meaning and sources of wellbeing.[24] Though there is a lot of debate on these matters, everyone agrees that the sources of wellbeing are diverse, interconnected and complex (figure 3).[25]

Wellbeing is a state of mind that reflects a set of complex relationships between material, relational, and subjective domains. This interplay must be understood as firmly located in society and shaped by social, economic, political, cultural and psychological processes.[26] Improving wellbeing requires at least as much focus on the processes followed as they do on the outcomes being

---
[23] OECD (2020), p17.
[24] Adler and Fleurbaey (2016).
[25] Reid (2019).
[26] Gough *et al*. (2007), McGregor (2007), White (2010).

Wellbeing and a radically different policy approach

Figure 3. Diverse and interconnected sources of human wellbeing

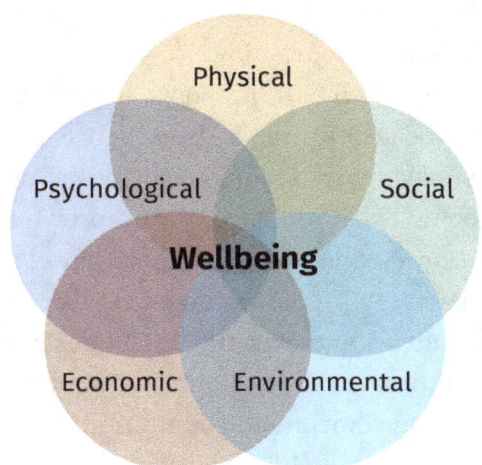

sought; indeed desired outcomes cannot be achieved unless the processes followed are genuinely and effectively inclusive.

This requires a balanced and integrated approach to public policy and management, across: the natural environment, society, and the economy; generations; society; the centre, regions, and communities; the big picture and the detail – a policy that sees the big picture but takes care of the detail as well.

Social context

The list of key dimensions of wellbeing in figure 1 relates to individual wellbeing. Needless to say, individual lives are lived in social settings. There are strong interdependencies between individual and community wellbeing.

As Kay and King (2020) explain, societies, communities and individuals have a very strong sense of what they value in life – the kind of lives they wish to live. Kay and King refer to these as 'reference narratives'. The major systemic risk that public policy needs to concern itself with is the threat to these reference narratives. If we can give people an assurance that their reference narratives will be protected, that provides a platform for creative explorations and human flourishing.

In addition, as Helliwell (2019) reports, social sources of wellbeing, especially those delivered in person, are of even greater importance for subjective wellbeing (one of the key dimensions of individual wellbeing listed in figure 1) than previously thought. In recent *World Happiness Reports*, six factors have been found to explain three-quarters of the differences in average life evaluations among countries and over time: GDP per capita; healthy life expectancy; and an additional four that can be described as social factors (having someone to count on in times of trouble; a sense of freedom to make life choices; generosity; and trustworthy environment, as proxied by the absence of corruption in business and government).

The largest gains come from the measure of social support. Within the *social*, the dominance of the *local* is of first-order importance – belonging, in an atmosphere of mutual support and trust. This goes far beyond being free from the risk of attack by others, as measured for example by fear of walking the streets at night, with remedies promised by the gated community; it is the capacity to feel embedded in a community where trust, belonging, and mutual support are the accepted norms.[27]

In short, if our purpose is to improve human lives as people wish to live their lives, then we need to place a lot of emphasis on the health and wellbeing of the communities in which those lives are lived.

In this context, the determinants of cooperative behaviour is most critical. Several studies show a very close link between the level of trust among the members of a community and the degree

---

[27] See also Santos (2020).

of cooperative and pro-social behaviours. In turn, individuals living in communities where trust and cooperation are high also experience higher levels of individual wellbeing.[28]

Radical uncertainty

We are trying to improve lives in a world dominated by *radical uncertainty*[29] and *adaptive complexity*.[30] In this type of world, which is the real world we are living in, there are no buttons to push that will generate well-defined outcomes. Which button would you push, for example, to 'solve' a mental health problem?

Under *radical (or fundamental) uncertainty*, with the set of possible states of the world and/or their probabilities unknown, optimisation at a public policy level (in the 'large world' as Kay and King (2020) label it) becomes impossible. While we may have a broad idea of the types of catastrophes our natural environment, society, and economy are most likely to be exposed to, we simply do not know what the future will look like.

We live in a world of radical uncertainty in which our understanding of the present is imperfect, our understanding of the future even more limited, and in which no one person or organisation can hold the range of information required to arrive at the best explanation. Narrative reasoning is the most powerful mechanism available for organising our imperfect knowledge. Understanding the complex world is a matter of constructing the best explanation – a narrative account – from a myriad of little details and the knowledge of context derived from personal experience and the experience of others.[31]

In the kind of world where we design and implement public

---

[28] See Carattini and Roesti (2020) for supporting evidence.
[29] Kay and King (2020), King (2016), chapter 4.
[30] Arthur (2014).
[31] Kay and King (2020), Kindle p6041.

policy, there is neither an optimal (or indeed maximal) solution we can jump to, nor a clear destination we can grope towards; there is complete uncertainty – both about future preferences and future possibilities. At a system level, the whole purpose of public policy is to create resilience towards unknown unknowns by investing in shock absorbing and creative capacities, so that current and future generations can survive and thrive.

Adaptive complexity
Under *adaptive complexity*, particularly in a social context, actions and outcomes cannot be separated. There is reflexivity: there are no external (exogenous) social or economic facts that are independent of our actions. Individuals' actions and interactions with others influence the social and economic outcomes that emerge, which in turn lead to reactions, and on it goes.[32]

One of the main teachings of complexity economics is that creative ideas are primarily generated bottom up – not top down – through interactions and cross-fertilisations of ideas promulgated by human contacts via various means. A critical role for the policy maker is that of supporting and connecting. Creativity remains the source of innovation, technological progress and prosperity under all frameworks – how we encourage and support it is the point of difference. Think of a landscaper instead of an architect; their focus is on creating the right ecosystems for people, communities and ideas to flourish.

---

[32] Soros (2003).

3. Public policy in a radically different world

How do we frame a wellbeing-focused public policy in a radically (or fundamentally) uncertain and complex world?

At a broader (system) level, such a framework would have three complementary dimensions. First, to create the environment (natural, social, and economic environment – the 'wellbeing garden') which makes the pursuit of valued lives possible (i.e. the *opportunities*). Second, to support the investments that provide individuals and communities with the *capabilities* to pursue their valued lives. Third, to shift the focus of policy from *direction* to *nourishment* – from looking for optimal solutions to well-defined problems to building resilience to unknown potential systemic risks that threaten valued ways of living, as well as encouraging creative responses through cooperative community mechanisms.[33]

In an intergenerational context, systemic resilience has three distinct but complementary attributes. First is shock-absorbing capacity (for example, following earthquakes, financial-system disruptions, or social disruptions); second is adaptability in the aftermath of shocks; third is creativity and inventiveness (which are critical ingredients of adaptability) – underpinned by individual freedoms and social cohesion.

In what follows, we take the messiness (that is, uncertainty

---

[33] See also Ostrom (2009).

and complexity) of the environment in which human lives are lived and public policy is implemented as a given. We then adopt the following foundational concepts and principles for a wellbeing-focused public policy – and follow them through consistently in our analysis and recommendations in this book.

First, wellbeing is associated with the capabilities and opportunities of individuals and communities to live the lives they value. Second, we respect the rights of individuals and communities to choose and live the lives they value. Third, valued lives are diverse, and are history-, time-, culture- and context-dependent. Fourth, lives are lived in social settings. Fifth, we want everyone to live the lives they value – provided they respect others' rights to do the same. Sixth, everyone includes future generations. Finally, the future is radically, or fundamentally, uncertain.

It follows that the broader environment in which wellbeing is attainable on a sustainable basis across generations would have the following characteristics. A natural environment conducive to human life, which means that environmental quality matters. Broader material and financial conditions need to be conducive to the pursuit of material prosperity. People have access to the rights and liberties (i.e. the personal freedoms) to choose and enjoy all aspects of their lives. They also need to have an effective voice, sharing the power to influence collective decisions. They need to experience safety and security. They need to be able to live together in peace and harmony with social cohesion. There needs to be equitable access to all the public-goods sources of wellbeing.

These are precisely the systemic outcomes that public policy needs to deliver. They represent some of the critical domains of public policy, and they can be delivered only through public policy because they each have very strong public good characteristics. Given the huge number of positive externalities associated with each, individuals or small communities will tend to under-invest in the sources of these public goods, which means that they will be under-provided.

To use a term that I learned from Othmar Winkler (2009), we need a 'macroscope' to bring the multiple developments in our natural environment, society and economy together so that we can see the big picture. This in turn helps us to develop frameworks for analysing and improving this picture. The wellbeing framework provides such a macroscope for public policy.

Figure 4 conceptualises the primary systemic purpose of a wellbeing-focused public policy as the enlargement of the wellbeing garden (or a wellbeing frontier), in which social life takes place, now and into the future. The perimeter of the wellbeing garden is defined by five posts that are tied together by a ribbon that surrounds them.

Moving clockwise, the first four posts represent the environmental, economic, political/legal and social outcomes (or opportunities) that underpin wellbeing. These are the key dimensions of the social and individual reference narratives, as Kay and King (2020) refer to them. The fifth post to which the ribbon is tied, represents the moral imperatives, in terms of equity and fairness (achieved by universal access to these outcomes), on which a wellbeing garden would be based. Thus, it is not only the availability of these first four outcomes that underpin sustained social wellbeing, but equal access to them by all members of society — which is what the aspiration of leaving no one behind is all about.

These are precisely the systemic outcomes that a wellbeing-focused public investment strategy would be pursuing. They provide the environment (natural, social, political/legal, economic, and moral foundations) which makes the pursuit of

Figure 4. Wellbeing garden

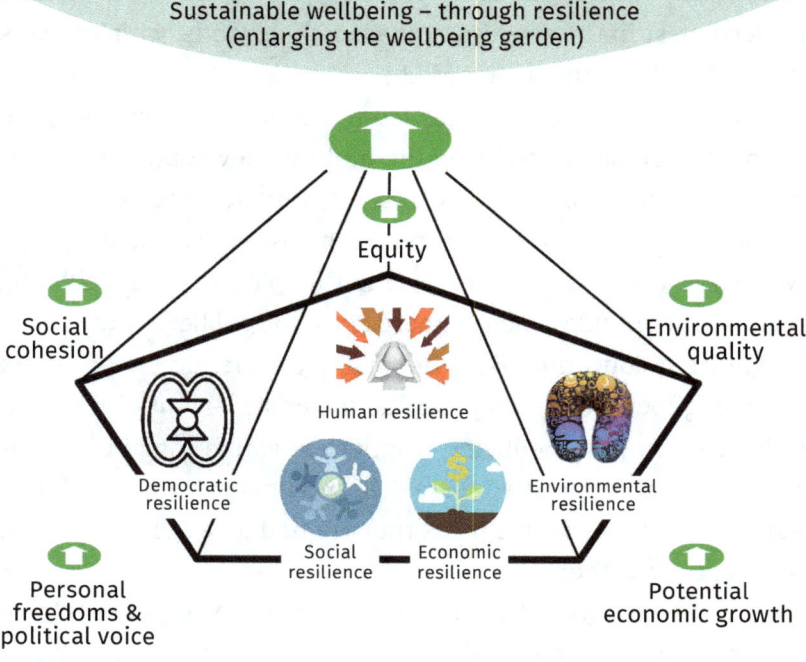

valued lives possible (i.e. the *opportunities*). The key focus of the strategy would be to invest towards building systemic resilience to potential threats to the key pillars that define the way we wish to live, to our reference narratives. The components of systemic resilience that sit in the middle of figure 4 provide individuals and communities with the capabilities to pursue their valued lives.

It is worth re-emphasising that all these pillars or posts that surround the wellbeing garden, thus defining its boundaries as well as representing the foundations of sustainable collective wellbeing, are strongly interdependent. By way of examples, if social cohesion collapses so too does potential economic growth.

If we cause serious harm to the natural environment, we end up compromising our economic growth potential. And so on. Our public investment decision environment should be strongly aware of these interdependencies, and deliberately exploit them in designing and implementing long-term public investments towards enlarging the wellbeing garden.

The critical policy question is this: what should the focus of these investment strategies be? With intergenerational wellbeing as our primary focus, and given the substantial uncertainty of the future, achieving *systemic resilience* emerges as a critical output of public policy. Investing in resilience provides the bridge to achieving sustainable intergenerational wellbeing in a world of fundamental uncertainty. By expanding the wellbeing garden we would also be enhancing the *resilience* of our society, now and in the future.

The key components of systemic resilience that we need to invest in, towards enlarging the wellbeing garden, are pictured in the middle of figure 4. In summary, investing in:

- *Social resilience* delivers social cohesion.
- *Human resilience* provides a major platform for equity.
- *Democratic resilience* underpins the protection of individual freedoms (rights and liberties) and political voice.
- *Economic and financial resilience* enhances potential economic growth.
- *Environmental resilience* helps sustain environmental quality.

In a decision environment of radical uncertainty, there are no optimisation problems to be 'solved'. Instead, there are safe and creative wellbeing gardens to be created through appropriate enhancements of the types of systemic resilience that sit in the middle of figure 4. What we have in mind are long-term investments in ecosystems (including institutions) that will provide a fertile ground for the outcomes that surround the wellbeing garden to emerge, and endure across generations.

Good strategies for a radically uncertain world acknowledge that we do not know what the future will hold. Such strategies imagine alternative future scenarios, and ensure that plans are robust and resilient to a range of plausible alternatives.[34] Radical uncertainty provides the opportunity for entrepreneurship, and is fundamental to an understanding of social, technological and economic progress.[35] If, through appropriate investments, we can somehow protect our way of life – our reference narrative – this would provide a safe platform from which we can launch our creative explorations towards flourishing. This is precisely what systemic resilience is meant to deliver.

'This new economic thinking may also provide the foundation for new political narratives. Eric Liu and Nick Hanauer, in their 2011 book *The gardens of democracy*, explore the possible shape of such a narrative. They liken the narratives of traditional economics to "machine-thinking" and advocate a shift to "garden-thinking" that emphasises the dynamic, constantly evolving nature of the economy, and the interconnectedness of society. The state then plays the role of a gardener helping create the conditions in which the garden of society can flourish.'[36]

This thinking and approach is also perfectly aligned with the Darwinian theory of evolution.[37] Darwin recognised the critical influence of environmental factors – in this case the natural environment – on the chances for the survival and thriving of species.

---

[34] Kay and King (2020), Kindle p6232.
[35] Ibid, p6342.
[36] Beinhocker (2016).
[37] Darwin (2003).

Here we are focused on identifying, and then deliberately investing in, the environmental, social, and economic ecosystems that support the surviving and thriving of individuals and communities.

As Sir Paul Nurse explains in his interview with Jim Mora on Radio New Zealand[38], there are five great ideas of biology that characterise living things. One of these is that all life evolves by natural selection; this is a way of living things acquiring purpose and excellent adaption to their environment and how they live without being designed – evolution by natural selection delivers purpose without design. Maybe God (the creator) created a system that could evolve in this way – a very beautiful mechanism – maybe more beautiful than the individual creation of lots and lots of different species. Or, as Carlos Rovelli puts it, 'There is no such thing as intentionality in nature. It isn't design that directs the combination of things, but it is the combination of things that gave rise to intentionality.'[39]

One could then imagine the distinctive role of public policy, in total alignment with the intent of Paul Nurse's creator, as setting up a social system that has the capacity to evolve, sustainably, into the indefinite future, without design, that is without predetermining the ultimate shape or destination of such an evolution. The primary focus of such a public policy would then be to ensure that human beings have the opportunities and capabilities to participate in, contribute to, and benefit from that evolution. The pillars that surround the wellbeing garden of figure 4 represent the key systemic ingredients of that social system, which collectively ensure the sustainability of wellbeing into the uncertain future – without any presumption that we can pre-design where it may head towards.

---

[38] Nurse (2020).
[39] Rovelli (2020), pp94–5.

How we undertake these investments is explored in some detail in chapter 5. Suffice it to emphasise at this stage, that there is no one-to-one relationship between investments in the capital stocks that sit at the bottom of figure 1 and the components of systemic resilience that sit in the middle of figure 4. In fact, investments in various types of capital will be required to deliver each type of systemic resilience. For example, delivering environmental resilience will require investments in natural capital, but also human capital (in the form of education), as well economic capital of the sort that operates with clean technology.

Even then, these foundations are necessary but not sufficient for delivering the desired wellbeing outcomes to the citizens. Consequently, the domain of public policy also includes governance and management processes for the effective delivery of these outcomes in an equitable and fair manner. This is where the role of communities becomes so important.

Once we decide to respect the rights of individuals and communities to choose and live the lives they value and acknowledge that valued lives are diverse, and are history-, time-, culture- and context-dependent, the *processes* we follow in designing, prioritising and implementing public policy become critical in achieving the ultimate *objectives* of public policy.

The degree of *inclusiveness* of these processes is of primary importance. The fact that individual and family lives are lived in social settings, and the imperative of social cohesion for sustainable wellbeing, makes the engagement of *communities* as full participants with the whole public policy and management process critical. We expand on this theme in chapter 6.

Welfare state vs wellbeing state
This is a good point to distinguish between a welfare state and a wellbeing state. This is a contentious matter from a purely eco-

nomic policy perspective, as going through the economics literature over many decades, one sees the terms welfare and wellbeing being used interchangeably; not always, but most of the time.

However, that is beside the point. There is in fact a fundamental difference between the mid-20th century 'entitlement state' (*welfare state*) and the early-21st century 'enablement and self-empowerment state' (*wellbeing state*).[40]

A welfare state focuses on delivering welfare itself, through redistribution of income and other direct sources of wellbeing, funded through taxation, social insurance or borrowing which will eventually need to be repaid through future taxation.

A wellbeing state, on the other hand, is focused on enabling individuals and communities to look after themselves through appropriate investments in the ecosystems that sit in the middle of figure 4, again funded with taxation and borrowing.

The role of a welfare state is to deliver welfare directly to those in need. Agency is typically assumed to reside with the government. A wellbeing state, on the other hand, aims to expand the opportunities and capabilities (i.e. substantial freedoms) of individuals to enhance their own wellbeing, underpinned by appropriate incentive structures. Its primary purpose is to enable the individuals and communities to live the lives they value.

Agency for improving wellbeing rests primarily with the individuals. The responsibility of citizens is to be actively engaged in pursuing what they want. Unless their circumstances make it inevitable, they cannot be passive recipients of what they value.[41] To the extent that welfare payments or support is required, it is strongly conditional on recipients' best efforts towards improving their lives.

---

[40] Cadogan (2013). [Italicised terms reflect my associations in the context of this book.]
[41] Dalziel and Saunders (2014), Sen (2009).

A wellbeing state is the steward on behalf of current and future generations of the ecosystems that underpin the types of systemic resilience represented in the middle of figure 4. While individuals do manage their own assets (including human capital), only a representative government can take a systems view, dealing with systemic risks and opportunities.

The evolution of public policy – or social policy to be more precise – over the centuries may also provide useful background and context to this distinction.

Broadly speaking, the aim of social policy is to improve people's lives. The most obvious way to do this is to lift people out of poverty, which is broadly defined as lack of access to what they need or value. It is to reduce and ultimately eliminate deprivation from the sources of wellbeing. The imperative of looking after the poor goes back 3,000 years and is a common theme across humanity, including Chinese, Christian, Hindu, Islamic and Jewish traditions.

A distinct additional, and possibly complementary, aim of social policy may be to improve the opportunities for people to live better lives. For example, this could be achieved through better access to education, health services, employment, housing and so on. It also involves removing inequities regarding such access across, say, genders, ethnicities, and age groups.

We can summarise the evolution of social policy in the industrialised economies of Europe (including the Scandinavian countries), the USA, the UK, Canada, Australia and New Zealand, using the parameters above as a prism. When we do that, we could broadly describe the evolution of social policy since the end of the 19th century as follows:[42]

- ♥ From being tax- (pay as you go) funded, to being social-insurance (save as you go) funded.

---

[42] Boston (2019), Cadogan (2013).

- From being primarily focused on helping the poor and needy, to adopting a widening welfare state role, and then towards adopting an enabling role.
- From individual responsibility, to broader state responsibility, back towards individual and family responsibility.
- From being universal, to becoming targeted (means-tested).
- From being a provider, to becoming an enabler.
- From an ideology of welfarism, to a wellbeing (social investment) focus.

Building on this broad-brush narrative:

> 'the basic regime changes in welfare can be briefly described as follows. The laissez faire liberal state can be identified as existing from its 1770s inceptions until the 1870s before another paradigm began to modify it, that of the dirigiste liberal state, which sought to "correct" capitalism, through regulatory instruments, and by establishing Government-Owned Companies (GOCs) and State-Owned Enterprises (SOEs).

> 'The main period of this post-classical liberalism in setting up the "enterprise state" and social provision state lay between the 1870s and the 1910s in countries ranging from the United Kingdom, to New Zealand, Germany, Austro-Hungary, United States state governments and Italy.'[43]

Welfarism is a much more modern concept. It represents a gradual:

> 'response of the liberal state to modernising industrial capitalist economies ... 19th century reactions to the Industrial Revolution were transformed into the mid-20th century welfare state. The brutal Poor Laws system became the late Victo-

---
[43] Cadogan (2013), p3.

rian and Edwardian pension or social insurance state, which in turn became the mid-20th century welfare state.

'The welfare state … came under review from the late 1970s in all OECD polities. The 1970s oil shock crises precipitated a profound review of the mixed economy state that brought about the emancipation of capital and of the markets that we know as neoliberalism. Prometheus was unbound.

'The welfare systems [were] made to do what they were arguably not set up to do: to provide long-term living standards support for large, unproductive sectors of the population and to subsidise the active economy. Instead of providing social safety nets to support the poor, the disabled and dependent, welfare states [were] converted into routine and universalised mechanisms of domestic economics. As infrastructure, they [became] the support systems for normal capitalist production. … The outright poor and unemployed and single mothers have been in constant hazard of stigmatisation.

'A marked shift has also occurred from the more utopian and therapeutic and "social engineering" aspirations of the mid-20th century towards the new governance and regulation of "responsibilitisation". Although a prolonged crisis has beset welfare provision in OECD nations since the financial crisis of 2008, the turn towards responsibilitisation is much older, dating from around 1990.

'Today, the sustainability and morality of publicly supported welfare systems are being debated pro and con at an intensity never experienced before. Opinion polls arguably show the greatest scepticism of welfare and antipathy to welfare recipients since the welfare state commenced.'[44]

---

[44] Cadogan (2013), pp3–4.

It is most important to note in this context that:

> 'In the early days of the European welfare state, social and economic policies were seen as working in the same direction. This view persisted for several decades. When, in the United Kingdom, Beveridge drew up his 1942 plan for postwar social security, he collaborated with Keynes to ensure that macroeconomic and social policy worked together, notably via the role of social transfers in providing automatic stabilisers.
>
> 'In the United States, Moses Abramovitz argued that "the support of income minima, health care, social insurance, and other elements of the welfare state, was [...] a part of the productivity growth process itself". Only later in the 1980s and 1990s, did the predominant view shift and come to see social protection as an impediment, rather than as a complement, to economic performance.'[45]

Following the 2017 general election, and faced with the realities depicted in table 1, we (in New Zealand) are now experimenting with what can be described as a wellbeing approach to social policy. The essence of this approach is empowerment and enablement through appropriate public investments; an enhanced version of the 'social investment approach' adopted by the 2008–17 National Party led government.

---

[45] Atkinson (2015), p265.

4. Resilience as a platform for sustained prosperity

In a world of substantive uncertainty, investing in resilience provides the critical bridge to the sustainability of wellbeing across generations. It is by investing in systemic resilience that we expand the wellbeing garden in an intergenerational setting. This can be achieved through appropriate, and complementary, public and private investments in the ecosystems that sit in the middle of figure 4 in chapter 3.

As already noted, in this context, wellbeing-resilience has two key and complementary dimensions – *surviving* and *thriving*. It is equity and fairness, in terms of having access to all forms of systemic resilience, that provide the glue to sustainability of wellbeing across generations.

Resilience can be usefully defined as the ability to prepare and plan for, absorb, recover from, and more successfully adapt to adverse events (National Research Council 2012). It refers to the capability of the economy and society to respond to significant systemic shocks, while continuing to operate reasonably effectively and efficiently in the aftermath – measured, in principle, in terms of the speed and cost of adaptation. A system may show resilience to major systemic shocks not necessarily by returning exactly to its previous state following a shock, but instead by finding different ways to carry out essential functions; that is, by adapting.

In an intergenerational context, systemic resilience has three distinct but complementary attributes: first is shock-absorbing capacity (for example following earthquakes, financial-system disruptions, or social disruptions); second is adaptability in the aftermath of shocks; and third is creativity and inventiveness (which are critical ingredients of adaptability), underpinned by individual freedoms and social cohesion.

To paraphrase North (1994), in a dynamic context, adaptive rather than allocative efficiency is the key to long run wellbeing. Successful economic, political, and social systems have evolved flexible institutional structures that can survive the shocks and changes that are part of successful evolution.

In a world of complexity and radical uncertainty, individuals and communities do not know the best course of action open to them. In fact, there is no objective, independent of our actions, best course of action to be discovered and implemented. Individuals constantly strive and experiment towards improving their lives or preserving the ways of living they value. The primary focus of policy then shifts to encouraging and incentivising individuals to continue doing so, while expanding the boundaries within which this ongoing experimentation takes place, as well as monitoring and ensuring that these boundaries are not crossed.[46]

Haldane (2018), partly based on the work of Broadberry and Wallis (2017), provides a very powerful and persuasive example of the interface between resilience, institutions, public policy, and wellbeing over a long period of time covering hundreds of years. This narrative is summarised in figures 5 and 6.

Here we see that the sustained growth in human prosperity

---

[46] Managing the system as a whole to ensure that critical boundaries are not crossed during adjustments to policy moves or to systemic shocks is the focus of 'viability theory' which we discuss and apply in a public policy context in Karacaoglu *et al.* (2019).

Figure 5. **Real GDP per head since 1000 CE**

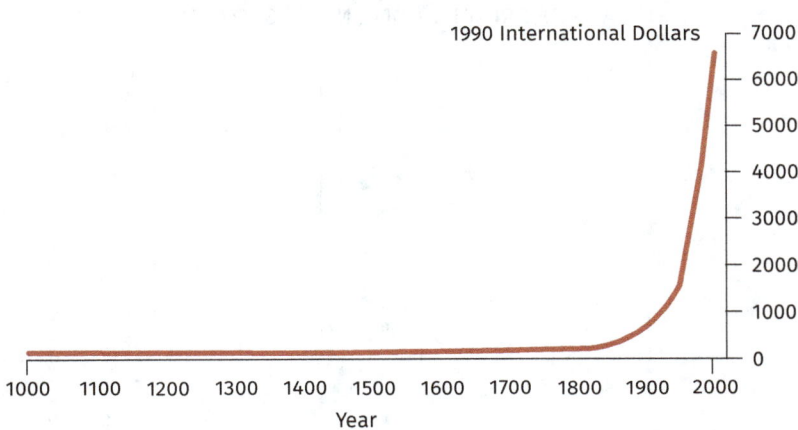

Sources: De Long (1998).

since the Industrial Revolution turns out to be not exclusively, or even primarily, an economic growth story underpinned by innovation and productivity growth – the standard narrative – but a resilience story as well. Growth spurts were ever present for at least a thousand years. Deliberately created social institutions such as schooling, health services, social welfare, that protected humanity from the potential negative effects of contractionary periods owing to war, disease, economic catastrophes and more, over the period since the Industrial Revolution, made a huge difference.

Adopting this new narrative, our proposed policy response to complexity and radical uncertainty is to expand the focus of policy from *direction* (where necessary) to also include *nourishment* as a contributor to building resilience to potential systemic risks that threaten our way of life, in other words our collective reference narrative.

The wellbeing garden of figure 4 can be enlarged through

Figure 6. Real GDP per head since 1000 CE

700 YEARS OF GROWTH / DECENNIAL GROWTH

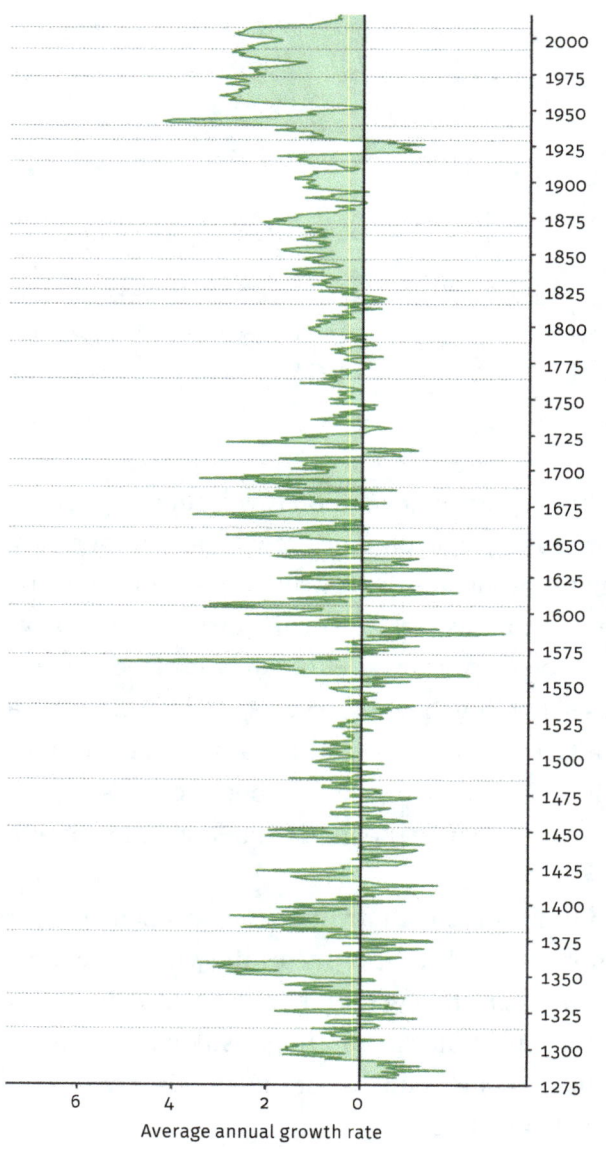

Sources: Broadberry and Wallis (2017) and Bank of England calculations.

appropriate (in terms of quantum, quality and composition) investments. The critical questions are: investments to *what end*, in *what*, and *how*?

Private and local investments are always taking place in the capital stocks that sit at the bottom of figure 1. Individuals and families are constantly investing in their own and their children's education and health (*human capital*); private companies are investing in factories, farms, land, financial institutions, and so on (*economic capital*); local governments and communities are investing in playgrounds, churches and all kinds of other sources of *social capital*; individuals, private businesses and local councils are investing towards cleaning waterways, lakes, and so on (*natural capital*).

Inevitably, all these investments in, for example, building schools and hospitals, involve various degrees of participation and contributions from, and are done in partnerships between, private individuals and businesses, local and regional governments, and central governments. There are very good reasons for this, economic and otherwise.

Here we are particularly focused on investments of a different and complementary nature, investments in broader infrastructures or ecosystems. What we have in mind are long-term investments in ecosystems (including institutions) that will provide a fertile ground for public good outcomes such as social cohesion and clean natural environment to emerge – and to endure. The existence of such ecosystems will also attract creative private investments that will attempt to exploit them for private gain, while also generating social benefits. For example, if private banks are to invest in a country, they want to see an established legal system, payments system, protection of property rights, as well as broadband and other related infrastructures. These are the types of investments to which we are referring.

Indeed, given our focus on expanding the wellbeing garden, the primary aim is to create the ecosystems that enable these other smaller investments to take place. This is the key insight of Mazzucato (2013, 2015): the public sector as the initial, pioneering investor and ecosystem creator in which the private sector, NGOs and others can find a fertile and profitable ground to invest in, and flourish. As Mazzucato points out, most of the radical, revolutionary innovations that have fuelled the dynamics of capitalism – from railroads to the internet, to nanotechnology and pharmaceuticals – trace the most courageous, early and capital-intensive entrepreneurial investments back to the state.

Sustainability
Figure 7 captures two main ideas. First, the interactions between various types of capital in generating sustained wellbeing. As Costanza *et al.* (2017), where we have borrowed this figure from, emphasise, it is the complex interactions between these various forms of capital assets that affect human wellbeing. Built capital and human capital are embedded in society, which is in turn embedded in the rest of nature.

Second, sustainability refers to the sustainability of human wellbeing, not necessarily to the sustainability or preservation of any particular form of natural capital. We should allow for the possibility of substitutability of various types of natural and other forms of capital in generating human wellbeing.

This last point is extremely contentious in the sustainability literature, and is at the heart of the intense debate between proponents of weak and strong sustainability. A very useful discussion of this distinction, including empirical evidence, is provided by Pelenc *et al.* (2015).

Under weak sustainability, we allow for a degree of substitut-

Figure 7. Sustainable human wellbeing

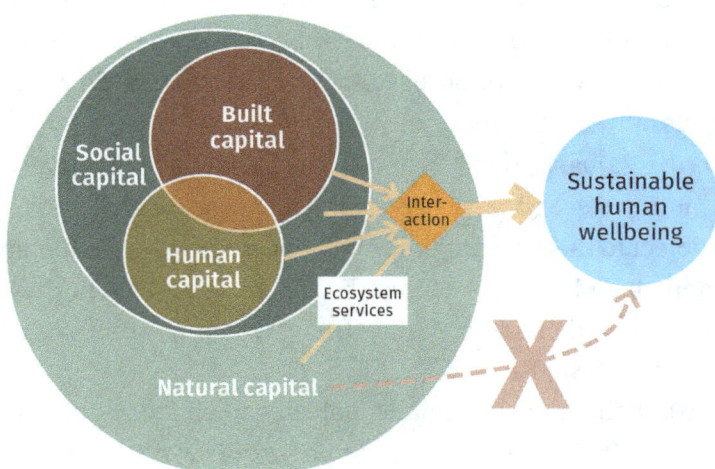

ability both within different categories of capital stocks (such as different elements of natural capital) and across them (such as between natural capital and human capital) in generating wellbeing. Under strong sustainability, at the very extreme all main categories of capital stock are pure complements in generating human wellbeing, with no substitutability allowed between them (although a degree of substitutability within each category may be allowed).

While in principle this is an empirical matter, in fact, it is very difficult to resolve it empirically. A practical and cautious approach, supported by Pelenc *et al*. (2015) as well, is to treat natural, social and economic ecosystems at large as complements – strong sustainability – while allowing substitutability at the margin within different categories of capital – weak sustainability – in the generation of human wellbeing.

Investing in systemic resilience

The crucial policy question then becomes: what are the critical ingredients of systemic resilience that could serve as a platform for sustained wellbeing across generations, and how do we invest towards enhancing them?

Let us go back to the proposition that most individuals and communities are constantly striving to pursue the lives they value, subject to their capabilities and opportunities (i.e. substantial freedoms), and conditioned by the incentives to which they are subject. They do so in social settings, which have strong reference narratives.

A wellbeing-focused public policy, imbedded in an uncertain and complex world, strives to first create the environment where the pursuit of valued lives is possible, and then support the acquisition of the capabilities and opportunities that enable the pursuit of these valued lives. It also ensures that this support is effective in improving all lives, leaving no one behind.

We suggested that the broader environment in which wellbeing is attainable on a sustainable basis, across generations, would have the following characteristics:

- A natural environment conducive to human life – hence, environmental quality matters.
- People are free to choose all aspects of their lives.
- They need to share the power to influence collective decisions – have an effective voice.
- They need to enjoy safety and security.
- They need to be able to live together in peace and harmony with social cohesion.
- There needs to be equitable access to all the public-goods sources of wellbeing.

💙 Broader material and financial conditions need to be conducive to the pursuit of material prosperity.

In this context, wellbeing resilience has two key and complementary dimensions – *surviving* and *thriving*. Equity and fairness, in terms of having access to all these forms of systemic resilience, provide the glue to sustainability of wellbeing across generations.

If we, through public policy and management, can give communities spread across the country the assurance that their way of life – their reference narrative – will be protected, this would provide them with the platform from which they can launch their explorations, be creative, thrive and flourish.

The critical dimensions of systemic resilience that would support the emergence of such an environment, conducive to sustainable wellbeing across generations, are: environmental, social, human, democratic, and economic (physical and financial).

We note that these – and not just narrowly defined capital stocks – sit in the middle of the wellbeing garden of figure 4. It is by enhancing these five categories of resilience that we expand the wellbeing garden.

For each one of these, the key steps in investing towards systemic resilience would involve trying to:

💙 Identify the key outputs that each of the critical ecosystems supporting intergenerational wellbeing delivers, as well as the potential catastrophes they are exposed to.

💙 Imagine the key systemic features that would, first, prevent such catastrophes from eventuating so that these key outputs continue to be delivered; second, absorb the shock so that the consequent damage is minimised if it were to take place; and third, support and facilitate a quick adaptation and recovery.

- 💙 Identify the key partnerships that would help create these systemic features, and involve them in reviewing and adjusting what we come up with in step 2.
- 💙 Collectively, explore and identify the types of interventions and investments (including the creation of institutions) that would bring about the systemic features identified in step 2.
- 💙 Make sure that the institutions established to deal with the fundamental systemic catastrophe are adaptable – that they have the capacity to evolve in response to the evolution of the environment in which they operate, including the impact of emerging technologies.
- 💙 Make sure that the presence of such institutions does not blunt the incentives of private individuals, businesses or communities to do the best they can for themselves, while internalising the consequences of their actions on others.
- 💙 Consider the complementarities between the outcomes of step 4, across all critical ecosystems.
- 💙 Prioritise and undertake the investments that are identified in step 4, while taking into consideration the complementarities identified in step 7.

Before demonstrating with examples how this would work (i.e. how these steps would be implemented) in practice, it needs to be emphasised that the common ingredients across all policy interventions we recommend towards enhancing these five types of systemic resilience, are *partnerships* and *institutions* (see chapter 6). And for these partnerships to work effectively and on an enduring basis, we need to build and maintain *trust* across all stakeholders.

Building resilience to the five critical systemic risks

We now turn to exploring how we can build resilience to the critical systemic risks we identified above – environmental, social, human, democratic, and economic – by following the steps in the previous section. In all cases, leadership and *partnerships* (based on a strong foundation of *trust*) will play a critical role in effective implementation. In some cases, such as those relating to the broader economic / financial system, central government would lead, while in others, such as those relating to social cohesion, local and regional government would take the lead. However, in all cases effective implementation will require engagement with *communities* and *strong partnerships* based on *mutual trust*.

Democratic resilience – curtailing power and privilege

One of the most important contributions that good institutions can make towards delivering sustained wellbeing across generations is to curtail power and privilege. Yet institutions are human-designed and created, and there will be a lot of pressure for creating and preserving the types of institutions that will serve the interests of the powerful. A broad and deep analysis of this dilemma, including a survey of associated ideas over millennia, is provided by Acemoglu and Robinson (2012, 2019).

Creating good institutions is the main vehicle through which a wellbeing state delivers good public policy. Good institutions are those that provide equal access to opportunities and capabilities to a broad cross-section of society. For such access to generate good environmental, social and economic outcomes, institutions need to also provide security of property rights.

Whether actual public policy pursues this purpose or not, and whose wellbeing is its focus, depends on the institutions that exist in a society. These institutions are the outcomes of social decisions, made by humans, chosen for their consequences; they reflect the evolution of the distribution of power in society. The distribution of power in turn is a reflection of the distribution of political and economic resources.[47]

Circumstances supporting good institutions are more likely to emerge when we have political institutions that place checks on those who hold political power; political power is broadly distributed and complemented by good investment opportunities; and when there are only limited rents that power holders can extract from the rest of society.

As the role of the state evolves, and possibly expands, taking on more responsibilities in a complex world, how do we ensure that it continues to serve, rather than dominate and suffocate, our freedoms and liberties? Based on English Philosopher John Locke's work, Acemoglu and Robinson (2019) associate liberty with 'people being free from violence, intimidation, and other demeaning acts. People must be able to make free choices about their lives and have the means to carry them out without the menace of unreasonable punishment or draconian social sanctions' (p. xii), also emphasising that no one ought to harm another in his life, health, liberty, or possessions (p. xi).

> 'For liberty to emerge and flourish, both state and society must be strong. A strong state is needed to control violence, enforce laws, and provide public services that are critical for a life in which people are empowered to make and pursue their choices. A strong, mobilised society is needed to control and shackle the strong state.'[48]

A great outcome would be for the state and its elites to learn to

---

[47] See Acemoglu *et al.* (2005), Acemoglu and Robinson (2012).
[48] p. xv.

live with the shackles that society puts on them. As well, different segments of society need to learn to work, live, and enjoy life together despite their differences – in other words enjoy strong *bridging capital* – a key component of social capital.[49] This requires mutually supporting interactions between governments (national, regional and local), communities and markets. The outcomes of policies should be thought of as ecosystems that facilitate such effective cooperation, including institutions.

One deliberate public investment to that end, strongly advocated by Rajan (2019), is to strengthen the communities through local empowerment (i.e. 'localism' – a topic we return to in chapter 6). This is totally aligned with the call of Banerjee and Duflo (2011, 2019) to complement the strong macro-level institutions that Acemoglu and Robinson (2012, 2019) strongly advocate as a platform for sustained liberty and prosperity, with local institutions that represent the cultures and idiosyncratic preferences of the various communities in which individual lives are lived.[50]

Resilience to systemic risks to the financial system

A proposal for public policy formulation and implementation when facing radical uncertainty and adaptive complexity is well developed by King (2016) in the context of monetary and financial policy.

An efficient and stable financial system is a critical ingredient of economic infrastructure as a platform for sustained overall wellbeing. How can public policy support an efficient and effective financial system, while at the same time ensuring sustainable financial stability by protecting it from potential catastrophes?

We are dealing with a complex system of intricately interre-

---

[49] Growiec *et al.* (2017).
[50] See chapter 6 in this book.

lated networks of financial institutions.⁵¹ These institutions play some critical roles, including: money creation (banks create deposits to finance risky lending), payments services, financial intermediation between borrowers and lenders, and maturity transformation (linking the present to the future).

This case is a useful demonstration of how the resilience-building steps identified above can be followed in managing this challenge.

As King (2016) convincingly argues, the main catastrophe the financial system, and through it the wider economic system, is exposed to is the drying up of liquidity for the whole financial system in a financial crisis (as it did in 2007/8). Avoidance of this type of systemic catastrophe through liquidity provision to the whole system is a critical public good.

Only central banks can perform this function, appropriately supported by key partners. In New Zealand, the key partners they should be working with in designing the system are the domestic private banking system, Australian parents of NZ's main banks, Australia's central bank (RBA), international financial organisations such as the IMF (International Monetary Fund), and members of CoFR (Council of Financial Regulators) such as the Financial Markets Authority (FMA), and New Zealand Treasury.

The main complementarities in this context are between monetary and fiscal stability/resilience and economic resilience.

How a central bank performs the function of ensuring access to liquidity for the financial system under all circumstances, and what incentives and constraints it wraps around it, is critical for the overall ongoing functioning of the system in an effective and efficient manner.

The way central banks have attempted to insure against

---

[51] See Haldane and May (2011).

financial catastrophe, by providing liquidity in an effective and efficient manner, has evolved over time. King argues that the traditional lender-of-last-resort (LOLR) mechanism for providing system liquidity has reached its use-by date, and it needs to be replaced by a pawnbroker-for-all seasons (PFAS) strategy, which he argues is a *coping* strategy in the face of radical uncertainty.

> 'The aim of the PFAS is threefold. First, to ensure that all deposits are backed by either actual cash or a guaranteed contingent claim on reserves in the central bank. Second, to ensure that the provision of liquidity insurance is mandatory and paid for upfront. Third, to design a system which in effect imposes a tax on the degree of negative externalities generated in our financial system – private financial intermediaries should bear the social costs of their actions.'[52]

In implementing this set of measures, we need to 'ensure that the risks involved in money and banking are correctly identified and borne by those who enjoy the benefits from our financial system'.[53] The measures we put in place should also ensure that, first, private institutions do internalise the wider (social) consequences of the risks they incur in the pursuit of profits, mainly through imposing higher equity ratios on their total assets; and second, that their creativity in using their balance sheets is not blunted through inappropriate regulations.

Since systemic risks cannot be privatised, we need to put measures in place to minimise their occurrence. These measures include, significantly higher capital adequacy ratios, leverage ratios, liquidity ratios, pre-insurance, and collateralisation. The technicalities associated with these terms need not dis-

---

[52] Ibid, p271.
[53] Ibid, p251.

tract us here. Suffice it to say, they are all measures targeted at making sure that the shock-absorbing capacity of the entire financial system as well as individual financial institutions are strengthened. Equally important is ensuring that these generic restrictions do not interfere with how financial institutions manage their balance sheets [assets (loans) and liabilities (deposits)]:

> 'We could leave the banks free to lend money as they please, provided we no longer allowed them to manufacture the money they lend. In short: nationalise money, but do not nationalise banking.'[54]

In the case of New Zealand, recent decisions to raise bank capital adequacy ratios, and the ongoing review of the Reserve Bank Act (including the review of bank resolution arrangements, and deposit insurance and depositor protection options) are examples of actions being taken, in consultation with all the key partners identified above, to strengthen both the stability and the resilience of the wider financial system.

Resilience to systemic risks to the natural environment
For environmental infrastructure and ecosystem services, the equivalents of liquidity (for the financial system) are the climate system and biodiversity.[55]

Climate warming and a gradual extinction of species diversity are the two sources of environmental disaster. This may be contested on the basis that it represents a very narrow perspective. There appears to be a broader consensus around the nine interlinked planetary boundaries identified by Rockström *et al.* (2009). This is not critical for our purposes; the approach advo-

---
[54] See Fisher (1936).
[55] De Perthuis and Jouvet (2015).

cated here can easily accommodate a broader range of critical systemic threats to environmental resilience.

Critical ingredients of the climate system and biodiversity are protected by natural regulatory systems needed for the reproduction (sustainability, viability) of natural capital stocks. The critical difference between financial and environmental ecosystems is that, in the case of the latter, once we breach the critical boundary(ies), there may be no turning back, so there needs to be a comparatively much greater focus on prevention (or mitigation) through appropriate policy interventions.

The key systemic features that would reduce the likelihood of a shock, absorb the shock so that the consequent damage is minimised if it were to take place, and support and facilitate a quick adaptation and recovery are, strong environmental/natural capital, strong culture of awareness of environmental risks, and lifestyles and production processes that minimise environmental damage.

The key partnerships that need to work extremely well in exploring and assessing options are, local/regional government, community groups (such as iwi), central government, NGOs; major economic actors (such as farmers and manufacturers).

The appropriate (and strongly complementary) policies come in three categories, just as they do with financial system risks. First, we need to make sure that we do not come anywhere near an environmental catastrophe. Second, and as a supporting precautionary measure, we need to ensure that all the complementary mechanisms are working to guide both consumption and production, towards products and services using cleaner technologies. Third, there needs to be genuine engagements with all key partners and stakeholders, assuring them that any major changes that are required will ensure just transitions.

We want to avoid an ecosystem collapse, in the form of an irreversible environmental disaster, in an effective, efficient, and equitable manner, taking into consideration both cross-society and intergenerational equity. Concurrently, we wish to use a suite of policy instruments to encourage the switch of both consumption and production towards clean products and services.

The set of policies that are aimed at keeping the ecosystem away from catastrophic boundaries are generically referred as prudential policies,[56] and typically have caps on various activities, such as emissions, as a critical ingredient. These caps are complemented by market mechanisms such as trading – thus cap and trade policies are common, as with emissions trading.

Prudential policies are policies that place a very high value on reducing the likelihood of a disastrous outcome, even if this is costly (in the short term) in terms of other objectives foregone. Such an approach is often advocated where there is great uncertainty about the conditions under which a disastrous outcome would occur.

Complementary incentive measures include large-scale deployment of environmental pricing (for example carbon price to deal with greenhouse gas emissions), R&D subsidies favouring the switch to clean technology, and taxes and other penalties against the use of dirty technology.

A critical ingredient is obtaining a political mandate for the external costs of development and production to be absorbed by those who reap most benefit. The obstacle is the interface between politics and vested interests. This is why education is such a critical ingredient of the solution; when people understand and insist on, say, a carbon tax, politicians will introduce it.

Equally important is an agreement on and strong and wide-

---

[56] Carlin and Bowles (2017), chapter 20.

spread support for just and viable transitions, a topic we will return to in chapter 8. Suffice it to say at this point, that all investments need to be tested against the sustainability constraint of not shrinking the wellbeing garden of figure 4. 'Justice' specifically refers to the equity or fairness dimension of that garden. 'Viability' refers to the desirability of not shrinking or pulling back any of the five dimensions of the garden, including the equity dimension.

In the very context of viable transitions, we need to look for integrated and mutually reinforcing environmental, social and economic solutions towards achieving sustainability, such as education, and poverty reduction. An example would be investing in ecosystems that support circular economies, complemented by local/regional investments that facilitate a switch to cleaner products and consumption, such as no plastic use.

Main complementarities are between environmental and economic resilience in particular – but also social resilience.

Resilience to systemic social risks

What would a catastrophe in, or collapse of, a social ecosystem be like? In recent times, Yugoslavia and Syria provide a flavour of the answer, and plenty of other examples exist across the world and throughout history. It results in the total collapse of the social order and disintegration of social cohesion.

The obvious systemic answer to immunising the social system for such a catastrophe is sustainable social cohesion, underpinned by heavy investment in *bridging capital*.[57] Specific policies towards that end need to be strongly grounded in the history, culture and values of the society one is living in. The lead should come from local governments and communities, appropriately funded and supported by the centre.

---

[57] Growiec *et al.* (2017).

In the New Zealand context, there are (historical) bicultural and (emergent) multicultural dimensions to ensuring social cohesion. In the Maori-Pakeha (European) bicultural context, social cohesion has been sustained through the recognition of and partial compensation for historical injustices, education, and a deliberate set of attempts to promote and imbed biculturalism. What also helps a lot in New Zealand's specific context is the role that sport, education, music and other social activities, play as catalysts towards building *bridging capital*.

What about the equivalents of market mechanisms and associated incentives that are so integral to solutions for economic, financial, and environmental stresses? Do they exist in the broader social sphere? The answer is yes, and it takes the form of strong and diverse communities. Coupled with economic prosperity and a sense of equity or fairness, these provide strong incentives for people to live in harmony.

To repeat, and to strongly re-emphasise, the glue that holds it all together is *trust*, within and between various groups of stakeholders.

Enhancing human resilience

The discussion of human resilience has deliberately been left to the end. Human resilience will benefit from improvements in all other types of resilience – natural environment, social, democratic, and economic. For obvious reasons, all of these will contribute to individuals' capabilities and opportunities to *survive* and/or *thrive* – the two dimensions of resilience.

In addition, giving all individuals access to good education, health services, basic amenities, housing and safety will have a direct positive impact on human resilience. Through that, it will also have a direct positive influence on equity – one of the primary pillars surrounding, and defining the boundaries of, the wellbeing garden.

In the context of just transitions, providing support in adjusting to major shocks, through various institutions such as unemployment benefits, job training, and support from labour unions, is a very valuable foundation for human resilience.

Protecting individuals from material poverty is another channel through which public policy can contribute to human resilience. Banerjee and Duflo (2011, 2019) explain in detail how cash, care, employment, and voice are the foundations of direct support towards supporting human resilience, when delivered in ways that respects human dignity.

Key partnerships associated with investing in human resilience are wide ranging. By way of examples, delivery of health and educational services will almost certainly require well-functioning partnerships (supported by mutual trust) between central and local government. Cash support will most probably come from central government, while care will be delivered at the community level. Employment can be provided through both national and regional programmes. Giving effective voice to everyone will certainly require active effort at both national and local level.

If our focus is on supporting both human *surviving* and *thriving*, the support of human resilience needs to be particularly sensitive to ensuring that the care and support provided does not blunt the incentives of human beings to look after themselves and their families. As Banerjee and Duflo (2019) highlight and document, this is intensely ideological territory. There is no strong evidence to support the view that supporting individuals to survive and thrive, disincentivises effort towards self-improvement.

5. Governing for intergenerational wellbeing

In a world dominated by radical uncertainty and adaptive complexity, a public policy that aspires to deliver sustainable wellbeing across generations as its primary *objective*, needs to deliver the five *outcomes* that surround the wellbeing frontier of figure 4 (environmental quality, potential economic growth – i.e. material sources of wellbeing, personal freedoms and political voice, social cohesion, and equity). These outcomes will be delivered through appropriate, and complementary, public and private investments in ecosystems that will enhance the types of resilience that sit in the middle of figure 4 in chapter 3.

The subject matter of this chapter is to elaborate on the governance infrastructure that would make all this happen. We argue that such a governance structure, to be effective and enduring, needs to deliver five critical *outputs*: *a long-term focus* in policy making; inclusive decision-making mechanisms that aggregate the wisdom, expertise, and experiences of all stakeholders – that is, effective and equitable *participation*; a suitable supporting *funding* infrastructure; institutions that enable and encourage, and indeed mandate, an *integrated environmental, social, and economic approach* to public policy; and *adaptive time consistency* – ongoing alignment of public policy with collective wellbeing, as the preferences of society evolve over time.

We conclude the chapter by noting that the components of

such a governance infrastructure are in operation in various countries around the world. Our plea and hope is that New Zealand should and can show the world how to implement this in a comprehensive and fully integrated way.

Safeguarding the future, supported by inclusive processes

The key components of a systemic governance regime that is focused on anticipating and safeguarding the long-term future have been laid out and discussed in detail in Boston (2017 a, b; 2019) and Boston *et al.* (2019). Figures 8 and 9 below, both borrowed from Boston (2017 a), provide an extremely useful representation of these elements.

This is great, all true, and extremely useful, but how do we give effect to it?

Assuming there is the political will, the steps to be followed are clear[58] – and every one of them is being implemented some-

Figure 8. Attributes of anticipatory governance

---

[58] See Boston *et al.* (2019).

Figure 9. Ways of improving anticipatory governance

where in the world (see below in this chapter). They are very much aligned with the steps advocated in figure 10 by Wallace (2019). This chapter also borrows several ideas from Warren (2019).

1. Clearly separate the short-term, three year management role of government from the long-term stewardship role of Parliament. The ongoing focus on separation of political *powers*[59] needs to be matched by an equally intense focus on the separation of political (including intergenerational) *responsibilities*.[60]

2. On behalf of the New Zealand public, current and future, Parliament specifies intergenerational wellbeing as the core objective of public policy. Through appropriate legislation, it declares that each government will be held accountable for

---

[59] See, e.g. Palmer and Butler (2016).
[60] As advocated by Boston (2017 a, b) and Boston *et al.* (2019).

Figure 10. Key characteristics of wellbeing laws

1 Define national wellbeing as social, economic and environmental	2 Commit the government to putting wellbeing at the centre	3 Place a duty on governments to consult on what makes a good society	4 Set out ways of working to support wellbeing
5 Require an annual report and ongoing monitoring	6 Locate power in an independent office for wellbeing	7 Put wellbeing assessments into the budget process	8 Set a timetable for reviewing

pursuing policies that promote this objective.

3. To operationalise step 2, Parliament sets the long-term environmental, social, and economic objectives and associated targets aligned with shared and sustainable, intergenerational wellbeing.

4. It does so under advice from an independent office for wellbeing (IOW) (mirroring the Parliamentary Commissioner for the Environment) – directly accountable to Parliament.

5. A multi-party, cross-Parliament, Parliamentary Governance Group (PGG) acts as the governance group for the IOW.

6. The distinctive role of the IOW is to monitor, on behalf of Parliament, progress towards the long-term wellbeing objectives that are prioritised. The IOW has the resources which are capable of assessing the long-term wellbeing impacts of the government's strategic investments.

7. In implementing steps 3 and 4, Parliament ensures, through appropriate collaborations with local and regional councils,

that regional and local voices are reflected in setting wellbeing objectives and priorities.

8. The implementation of steps 3 and 4 is also informed by inputs from a *What works wellbeing* network of NGOs, local and regional government representatives, academics, and so on, working collaboratively to generate policy-informing ideas based on engagements with communities and research – like the UK model referred to in figure 11.[61]

9. Parliament legislates that the government will set short-term targets towards achieving the long-term targets set under step 3 and, each year, as part of its annual budget, will provide a report on how it is progressing against those targets.

10. Both the long-term monitoring by the IOW (see step 6), and the short-term policies and reporting undertaken by the government under step 9, will refer not only to national averages but also to the distribution of various wellbeing measures across various segments of society.

Figure 11. What Works Network – UK

What Works Centre for Wellbeing

An independent, collaborative organisation set up to develop and share robust, accessible and useful evidence about wellbeing.

We want a future where the wellbeing of people and communities improves year on year and wellbeing inequalities are reduced.

We develop and share useful evidence that governments, businesses, communities and people can use to improve wellbeing across the UK.

We believe that improving wellbeing should be the ultimate objective of policy and community actions.

---

[61] Hey (2019).

11. A dedicated investment manager associated with each long-term outcome – such as child poverty – and reporting to the IOW, plays the public sector stewardship role. Cost-benefit (or more specifically cost-wellbeing) analyses, using wellbeing as the currency, provides the main analytical tool for the interactions between these investment managers and the IOW.[62]

12. Where it is deemed appropriate by the IOW that the delivery of a certain long-term outcome requires substantive community ownership and participation in the achievement of that outcome, a community-based manager and budget holder (typically part of local/regional government), accountable to the IOW, is established.

It is clear from the governance structure outlined above, that the successful pursuit of long-term objectives requires the establishment of critical partnerships, based on mutual trust, between Parliament, the government, ministries, and local and regional government, as well as other stakeholders such as businesses, scientists, academics and so on. The proposed governance process also acknowledges the role of communities in effective governance towards intergenerational wellbeing. This role is institutionalised by making sure that the voices of the communities are reflected in the wellbeing objectives, priorities, and targets set at local and regional levels.

Funding

How should such long-term investments be funded? There is a critical nexus between finance and sustained development, which provides a distinctive role for public policy. Innovation-supporting investment needs a long-term commitment, supported by

---

[62] See Adler and Fleurbaey (2016), Fujiwara and Dolan (2016), Frijter *et al.* (2019), Jara and Schokkaert (2016).

patient finance, as well as an appetite for risk-taking in the face of radical uncertainty.

This is especially the case when we are talking about transformative infrastructure investments, such as those supporting green growth, nanotechnology, biotechnology, and so on. These are the circumstances when the state needs to lead (and has historically done so); only then does the private sector, including venture capital, follow.[63]

In a similar vein, Campiglio (2016) adds:

'In order to carry out their activities, low-carbon firms necessitate credit. Under certain economic conditions, of which the post financial crisis period represents the most recent realisation, banks may lack the confidence to create new credit even in the presence of right prices and profitable investments. This credit market failure, together with the deep uncertainties surrounding the future implementation of a carbon price, makes the case for considering a wider portfolio of policies.

'Examples include green differentiated reserve and capital requirements, modifying the risk weights for computing capital requirements in favour of low-carbon assets and other quantitative macroprudential policies aimed at easing lending conditions for low-carbon firms.'[64]

Long-term investments in ecosystems are eventually funded through taxes or levies – pay as you go (PAYGO), or social insurance (i.e. public saving in various forms to fund future needs and contingencies) – save as you go (SAYGO). An interim funding mechanism may be to borrow and pay, but both the principal

---

[63] Mazzucato and Wray (2015); Mazzucato and Perez (2014); Mazzucato and Semienuk (2018).
[64] p227.

of the debt and interest accrued on it will eventually be funded through PAYGO or SAYGO mechanisms.

We know that if the real return on capital is higher than the real growth rate of the economy, funding long-term investment expenditures via SAYGO is intergenerationally more efficient and equitable than doing so via PAYGO.[65] In New Zealand, SAYGO machinery has already been established in the form of the NZ Superannuation Fund. This would provide an excellent vehicle for funding investments by enhancing the resilience of key infrastructures.

Funding would be provided through a strategic portfolio allocation (say 20 percent) from the NZ Superannuation Fund. To accommodate this, the NZ Superannuation and Retirement Income Act 2001 would need to be amended to include a clause to the effect that 'The Fund remains a long-term, growth-oriented, global investment fund. However, its strategic portfolio allocation recognises that its reason for being is broader than simply funding superannuation, but also includes all long-term, wellbeing oriented, investment activities of the state.'

It is critical that the private sector is brought in as a partner and co-investor in infrastructure projects, participating in the selection of investments, their funding, as well as in managing associated risks:

> 'There are a number of models that can be adapted for new infrastructure projects. The Government has already begun work on coordinating the infrastructure pipeline and finding new ways to unlock private sector investment in infrastructure delivery. For example, the Infrastructure Funding and Financing Act 2020 (IFF) offers a new model for the provision

---

[65] Evans *et al.* (2013), p. ii.

of housing and urban development using special purpose vehicles to raise finance for new or upgraded infrastructure, with the cost paid, over time, through the rates system.

One successful model used offshore is the co-investment model, where a Government agency invests alongside the private sector. An example of this is the mutual investment model adopted in Wales. The structure is based on a public private partnership but with a Government agency investing in the special purpose vehicle alongside the private sector. Another example is an infrastructure bank that unlocks co-investment from the private sector.

This approach ties in nicely with the Government's focus on climate change. There are a number of examples overseas of a government-sponsored investor being established to grow the green investment sector in partnership with the private sector. In the last term, the Government took some initial steps in this direction by establishing Green Investment Finance to catalyse the development of a green investment market and facilitate private investment. There is a great deal of experience and expertise in the private sector in structuring and funding new renewable energy projects (including wind and solar in Australia) that can be harnessed to help achieve New Zealand's development of new renewable generation and electrification of transport networks.'[66]

Once long-term investment priorities are determined and approved by Parliament, the management of the budget would work as depicted in figure 12.

Any funding allocation to local and regional projects would

---

[66] Hunt and Peachey (2020).

be managed through the community-based manager and budget holder (typically part of local/regional government), accountable to the IOW, referred to in step 12 under governance. Targets, timelines and budgets would be confirmed, and ongoing funding would be conditional on delivery against these targets. The allocation of funding would also be conditional on the processes being followed to give voice to the community in setting priorities for budget bids.

There is another issue that is distinct but extremely relevant in the current context. If we are going to fund collective expenditures undertaken by government through taxes, what type of tax is most appropriate – i.e. meets all three of the effectiveness, efficiency and intergenerational equity criteria? I will answer this question with an example to illustrate the types of conversations we need to be having as a society if we take the public policy objective of intergenerational wellbeing seriously.

In chapter 8, I make a case on grounds of both fairness and equity (both intra- and intergenerational equity) for providing each child from a low income/wealth family (in other words, it will be means-tested), with an investment fund at birth, to be accessed when they reach the age of 18, for specific uses, such as education, establishing a business or buying a home.

I suggest that, to that end, we establish a *NZ Children's Fund*, which is to be the equivalent of our *NZ Super Fund*. The Fund would be funded through a land tax levied on the value of unimproved land. As we already have a land tax in New Zealand, the tax rate would have to be raised for this purpose. As Coleman (2018) carefully explains, a land tax is effective (hard to avoid), efficient (causes minimum distortions in decisions relating to the allocation of economic resources), and intergenerationally equitable (partly through lower house prices, it transfers resources from current to future generations).

| Governing for intergenerational wellbeing

Figure 12. Traditional and wellbeing budget processes

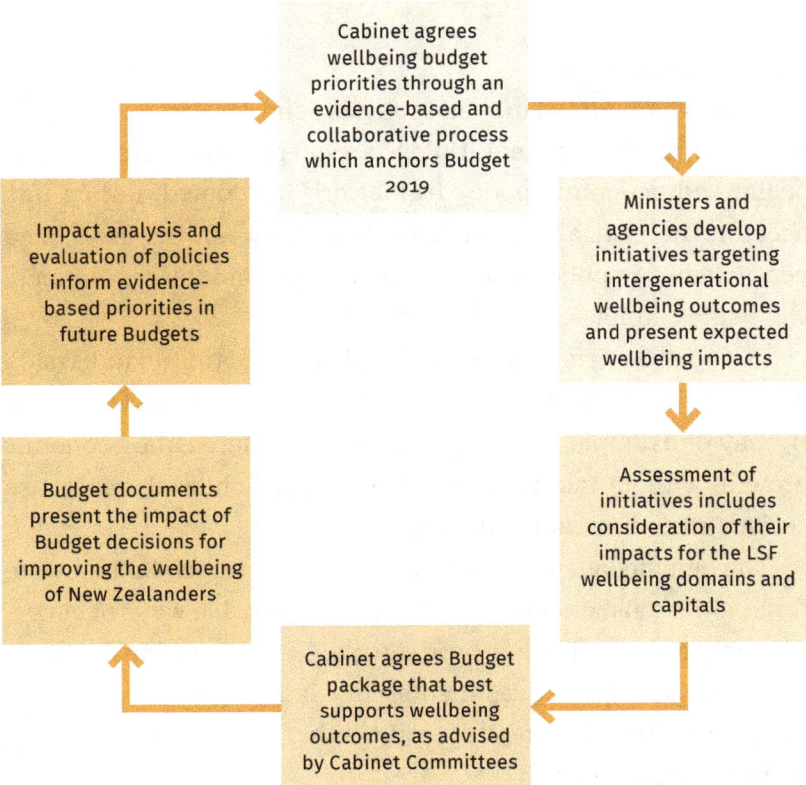

Source: Robertson, 2019, figure 1, p.4.

Furthermore, to generate support for such a tax, we would make it a hypothecated (or ring-fenced or earmarked) tax, dedicating the revenue from it specifically and exclusively for the purpose of funding the *NZ Children's Fund*. Such a proposal may prove to be palatable to the land-owning part of the population if they believe and *trust* that this will genuinely improve the life-chances of young people from low-income/wealth families.[67]

Establishing such an infrastructure is an example of the deliberate creation of an institution specifically targeted to building trust, through transparency and accountability, for serving a highly desirable social purpose.

Integrated approach

Human lives are lived in social settings, and society is embedded in a natural environment. Unless an integrated environmental, social and economic policy framework is adopted, taking into account the critical interdependencies between the associated ecosystems, a public policy that is focused on intergenerational wellbeing cannot achieve its objective.

The costs and risks associated with not adopting an integrated approach is the potential harm to the sustainability of wellbeing. By way of example, an excessive focus on increasing economic growth, without taking care of how this is achieved, can cause serious environmental damage.

The benefits of adopting an integrated approach boil down to finding the most effective, efficient and equitable ways of generating sustained wellbeing, by identifying and exploiting the interdependencies of key investments. For example, reducing poverty has positive benefits on all five pillars that define the boundaries of the wellbeing garden.

---

[67] See also Ryan Greenaway-McGrevy, Ryan, *et al.* (2020).

The imperative for adopting an integrated approach is grounded in the impossibility of finding silver bullets for achieving sustainable wellbeing across generations. Rather, we need to think of complementary policies of the sort explored in chapter 8. In anticipation of that discussion, and only by way of example, consider a focus on improving mental health, and suppose that we do make progress towards achieving it for some.

This would certainly increase the wellbeing of those individuals directly. It would also contribute to their wellbeing indirectly, by making them more productive, thus capable of earning higher incomes. If we stop there, however, these higher incomes will be spent on higher consumption, generating higher economic activity and causing increased pollution. One way of addressing this dilemma would be to complement policies aimed at improving mental health with those that switch both production and consumption towards more environmentally-friendly products.

Adaptive time consistency

'Time consistent policies are not policies that are never changed, but policies where any changes required by new circumstances are consistent with maintaining the original purposes of the policy. They are important for the socially desirable performance of the private and public sectors. This is because they provide stability that enables individuals and the state to plan for the future.

'We argue that time consistency is achievable if intergenerational arrangements between the state and the populace are treated as relational contracts. A relational contract is quite different from a legal contract since the latter typically imposes specific constraints on arrangements. A relational contract does not define specific constraints but rather a process for developing and changing rules by which all parties agree to abide".[68]

A very good example of time-consistent policies is provided by the rules, including voting thresholds, that countries impose for making changes in their constitutions.

This is why democratic institutions are so critical in helping us resolve tensions through public reasoning and deliberation.[69] The democratic process, in the form of representative democracy, supported by appropriate institutions, provides the forces that push towards an alignment of collective action (implemented through the government as our agent) with evolving private and communal interests.

To paraphrase North (1994), in a dynamic context, it is adaptive rather than allocative efficiency that is the key to long run wellbeing. Successful economic, political, and social systems have evolved flexible institutional structures that can survive the shocks and changes that are part of successful evolution. This ensures time consistency.

International benchmarks and examples

Are the suggestions made so far pie in the sky? Not at all. In fact, most of the suggestions provided above, in relation to governance and funding, are being implemented somewhere in the world. This means that they cannot be dismissed as academic or impractical. The only question is, do we have the conviction and the will to emulate others who are succeeding?

Denmark is one of the countries that sets a benchmark worth emulating. 'For many modern Europeans, Denmark was "number one" – rich, socially cohesive, with enviable infrastructure

---

[68] Evans *et al.* (2013), p. ii.
[69] See Bertram and Terry (2013), Sen (2009), Walzer (1983).

Governing for intergenerational wellbeing

and environmental standards – and it regularly features near the top in surveys of the world's happiest populations. "Hygge", sometimes defined as "cosy contentment and well-being through enjoying the simple things in life", has recently become one of the few Danish words to enter the English language.[70] ... The people of Denmark or Switzerland can enjoy uncertainty because they experience little risk and are secure in their reference narratives.'[71]

A second example is Finland. One of the explanations provided as to why Finland is the 'happiest country in the world'[72] is that people who live there are broadly content with their lives. The rich are less rich, the poor are less poor; everyone matters and feel valued; by and large everyone has the same sort of treatment; they think they have good schools; they believe they have good hospitals; everyone goes to those good schools and good hospitals; there is fair play; things are fairly done; there is therefore less envy and less anger and less resentment.[73]

A few more examples follow. Of course, they are illustrative only, not exhaustive.

- ♥ Bhutan is a country that has made wellbeing the primary objective of public policy; it has recognised the critical influences of environmental, social and economic factors on wellbeing; and it has developed and is applying a Gross Happiness Index (GHI) in designing, evaluating, and monitoring the success of public policies.[74]

- ♥ The Scandinavian countries – Denmark, Finland, Norway,

---
[70] Kay and King (2020), Kindle edition. p6265.
[71] Ibid., p6292.
[72] Helliwell *et al.* (2019).
[73] Morpurgo (2020).
[74] Tobgay (2016).

Sweden – which consistently rank highly on international wellbeing comparisons, have put a lot of emphasis on equity and fairness in the design and implementation of their public policies.[75]

- Several OECD countries are closely monitoring the progress of wellbeing, as well as economic indicators, in assessing public policy – and are actively pursuing inclusive growth strategies.[76]
- The Netherlands, among others, has established an independent and publicly-funded institution to assess the broader impacts of proposed public policies, and has independent reporting of such progress.[77]
- The Netherlands also has a 'circular economy by 2050' programme.[78]
- In Australia, the government has been exploring the idea of establishing an Evaluator General, situated within the Department of Treasury (not an independent institution), to assess/evaluate proposed social and economic investment programmes.[79]
- In Wales, the Wellbeing of Future Generations Act (2015) has established a *Future Generations Commissioner* as a guardian of the interests of future generations.[80] Among other activities, they are empowered to undertake independent reviews of public policy actions.[81]
- In the United Kingdom, a *What Works Wellbeing* network has

---

[75] Investopedia (2019).
[76] OECD (2019).
[77] Stoel (2019).
[78] Government of the Netherlands (2016).
[79] See Dennett (2018) for a brief overview.
[80] See also the proposal of Agar (2020) in this context.
[81] Future Generations Commissioner, Wales (2020).

been established to provide evidence-informed suggestions on how to improve lives. It is based on strong collaboration among various groups and agencies, and is partly publicly funded.[82]

- The United Kingdom Green Book (HM Treasury 2018) provides central government guidance on the appraisal and evaluation of public sector projects, using a broad spectrum of criteria.
- The United Arab Emirates (UAE) appointed a Minister of State for Happiness and launched the National Programme for Happiness and Positivity.[83]

OECD (2019) electronic presentations are publicly available and provide numerous other examples of very exciting initiatives towards designing, implementing, and evaluating wellbeing-based public policies.

To be fair, New Zealand is not standing still. The OECD (2019) review notes, with approval, that 'Improving the well-being of New Zealanders and their families is one of three strategic priorities for the [NZ] government. Their broad programme includes amending legislation to embed well-being objective-setting and reporting; developing well-being frameworks and indicator sets; and using well-being evidence to inform budget priority-setting and decision making, including by embedding well-being analysis in policy tools.'[84]

The same review also highlights that a wellbeing approach to public policy is being implemented:[85]

- 'Building on many years of work, the Treasury has recently updated its Living Standards Framework and released a Dashboard for measuring and reporting on well-being.

---

[82] Hey (2019).
[83] United Arab Emirates (2017).
[84] p2.
[85] Ibid., p4.

- The concepts and indicators included in the Dashboard are generally well-aligned with those measured in other countries, but there are gaps, including in some aspects of natural capital where New Zealand has experienced some downward trends or fares poorly.

- Work to address these gaps is ongoing, and a more comprehensive database (Indicators Aotearoa New Zealand) is being developed by Stats NZ.

- Five priorities were agreed for the 2019 Budget using well-being evidence. All agencies seeking funding for new initiatives were expected to identify well-being impacts.

- The Treasury's cost-benefit analysis tool has been updated to link impacts to well-being domains and can be used as a supporting tool for developing budget bids.

- Priority was given to initiatives that align with the budget priorities and show cross-agency and cross-portfolio collaboration. The government is also considering options for embedding a well-being approach in legislation.

- The latest proposals for the Public Finance Act would require governments to set well-being objectives and report on them annually, while the Treasury would report on well-being every four years. This follows the passing of the Child Poverty Reduction Act in 2018, which put into law the requirement to have both measures of and targets for child poverty.'

We can add some others to the list.

It is good to see that under the new, 2020, Labour Government, the finance and infrastructure portfolios are overseen by the same Minister, who also happens to be one of the main champions of the wellbeing approach to public policy. This provides a great opportunity for adopting an integrated governance approach to wellbeing policy, as outlined above.

Pursuing the 'four well-beings framework', the Local Government (Community Well-being) Amendment Act 2019 (LGAA 2019) has reinstated the promotion of social, economic, environmental and cultural wellbeing of communities to the statutory purpose of local government. Under this Act, the local authorities have to take into account 'the likely impact of any decision on each aspect of well-being' (cl. 7).

The Social Wellbeing Agency (the former Social Investment Agency) has a broad programme of work that is exclusively focused on using data and analytics to inform social policy.[86]

The Impact Lab, along the lines of *What Works Wellbeing* in the UK, based on global and local research and evidence, and lived experiences, identifies social interventions that have a positive impact on improving lives.[87]

In a similar vein, institutions such as Transition-HQ[88] are emphasising the importance of not violating critical environmental / climate constraints in designing and implementing public policies.[89]

We have several, informal, cross-party groups of Members of Parliament (MPs) advocating for various positive social outcomes, such as improving mental health.[90]

While all this is extremely encouraging and promising, one of the most important lessons we still have to learn from the world, especially from the likes of the *What Works Wellbeing* approach, is the critical importance of evidence-informed *delivery* (that is, *out-*

---

[86] https://www.govt.nz/organisations/social-wellbeing-agency
[87] https://impactlab.co.nz
[88] https://www.thq.nz
[89] Also see Krumdieck (2020).
[90] Alexander (2019).

comes), as distinct from and a complement to evidence-informed *policy*.

In this context, the work of the Impact Lab, referred to above, is most encouraging. Their primary purpose and motivation are to identify initiatives, grounded in communities spread around the country, that are actually making a positive difference in people's lives, with a view to raising funds for them.

On a broader, systemic, scale, having well-designed governance structures are essential, but they are not sufficient. Someone has to actually *do* what has been decided (think of the failure of KiwiBuild) and deliver the critical outputs that are essential to achieving the environmental, social and economic outcomes that have been prioritised. We need to reinstitute a version of the Ministry of Works and Development (the Department of Public Works), which was founded in 1876, and disestablished and privatised in 1988,[91] to coordinate, with private sector and local/regional partners as required, and implement the infrastructure projects.

Equally important, and to repeat, is the importance of taking into account the critical constraints (those that surround the wellbeing garden of figure 4) in the prioritisation, design and implementation of public policies.

Another critical lesson is that the *process* followed in both designing and implementing public policy matters for the achievement of enduring environmental, social and economic outcomes. The more inclusive the process, the higher the likelihood of an enduring positive outcome for sustained wellbeing.[92]

Also not to be forgotten, based on examples provided by Denmark and Switzerland, is the importance of making the protec-

---

[91] Wikipedia (2020).
[92] OECD (2019 (b)).

tion of the national reference narrative – how people want to live and what they value most about their lives – a major focus of our wellbeing strategy, through investing in resilience. That provides the platform for these countries' success in flourishing through creativity, underpinned by the assurance that their way of life will be protected through effective risk management.

Finally, and following from the points made above, the assessment of public policy, that is its evaluation, should also be outcomes (or delivery) based.

6. Inclusive processes required for sustainable wellbeing

In the previous chapter we argued that one of the critical outputs that wellbeing-focused governance arrangements need to deliver is inclusive decision-making mechanisms that aggregate the wisdom, expertise and experience of all stakeholders to inform the end-to-end policy approach. In this chapter, after a brief discussion of *participatory development*, we explore the role of institutions in public policy when wellbeing is the objective, and explore the types of institutions that are most conducive to achieving inclusive processes towards that objective.

The fact that individual and family lives are lived in social settings, and the imperative of social cohesion for sustainable wellbeing, makes the engagement of communities as full participants in the end-to-end public policy and management process critical. 'Policies aimed to improve people's quality of life need to include their experiences, aspirations, and priorities.'[93] This provides the crucial link between the *participatory* and *capabilities* approaches to public policy.

Participatory development[94]

Participatory development views the recipients of development as being at the forefront of, and actively involved in, decisions that

---

[93] Reid (2019), p44.
[94] This section is substantially based on Reid (2019).

affect their lives. Wellbeing priorities are defined by the communities. Public policy operates at the system level and ensures that communities have the resources and the voice to give effect to these priorities, calling on help and support from the centre as required.

Early promoters of this field were Freire (1970), and Fals-Borda and Rahman (1991), who were involved in what Hickey and Mohan (2004) termed emancipatory participation. They advocated for methods that incorporated the perspectives of local residents in the research and planning phases of development, principally through participatory action research (PAR), and emphasised the political nature of participation as a struggle against political, social, and economic exclusion.

The importance of participatory theory and practice to wellbeing is its attention to, and critical engagement with, power, politics and context. Prioritising wellbeing at the local level, as a participatory approach would do, legitimises discourse that would otherwise be overlooked in top-down frameworks, refocusing our attention on whose wellbeing is being promoted and in what ways.

The World Bank's Poverty Reduction Group used participatory approaches to determine the selection of quality-of-life domains in their *Voices of the poor project*.[95] Collecting over 60,000 voices from 60 countries, three volumes discussed well-being and ill-being from the perspective of poor communities. The key themes that emerged from the findings were the central importance of people's agency and capabilities, and the fact that wellbeing was viewed multidimensionally, not just in terms of income.

Scott (2012) notes that local conceptualisations of wellbeing, forged through an active process of debate and discussion,

---

[95] See Narayan *et al.* (2000).

Inclusive processes required for sustainable wellbeing

encourage more locally appropriate policies and increase capacity to address the complexities involved in assessing wellbeing at the community level. Research by Dorn *et al.* (2007) suggests that participation of this kind is linked with an increase in subjective wellbeing (SWB) because it is likely to produce political outcomes that are closer to people's preferences.

This also highlights the critical links between participatory and capabilities approaches to wellbeing. At the heart of the capabilities approach is an assessment of people's freedom and agency. Sen (1996) writes that a focus on development without freedom is incomplete: 'the "good life" is partly a life of genuine choice, and not one in which the person is forced into a particular life – however rich it might be in other respects'.[96]

Some complementarities emerge at the intersection of participatory research and the capability approach. To begin with, the use of participatory methods is essential to the successful application of the capability approach. Sen (1999) notes the fundamental importance of public debate and deliberate participation in the process of choosing the dimensions of wellbeing.

This sentiment is echoed by Alkire (2005). 'If the capability approach is applied in a way that is consistent with its own tenets, then its operationalisation depends upon the thoughtful participation of many users and much public debate. For that reason, the capability approach is very conducive to participatory undertakings.'[97]

Alkire (2002) lists four commonalities between the two approaches:

- 💚 the purpose of participation is to obtain outcomes that people value while also directly supporting empowering choices;

---
[96] p59.
[97] p218.

- they both consider the issue of 'who decides' as important as 'what is decided';
- they recognise that there may be no best choice, but that discussion offers an effective means of separating better from worse choices; and
- they both promote reasoned deliberation as a valid method for evaluating and making policy.

So, what would a participatory approach to public policy that is focused on building resilience to unknown systemic shocks look like? How would it be framed? How would it be implemented so that adaptive complexity is taken into consideration as well? The foundations of such a policy would include:[98]

- a recognition of the limits of what we are likely to know about a complex and functioning order;
- a recognition that individuals and communities will respond and adapt to whatever changes are put in place;
- the contributions to resilience of social, natural, regional diversity;
- the indispensable role of practical knowledge, informal processes and improvisation in the face of unpredictability;
- an appreciation of the complementary roles of the centre and the local/regional communities; and, in that very context,
- the advantage that the centre has in seeing the big picture, identifying trends early, and intervening in a timely fashion in epidemics.

One of the main teachings of complexity economics is that cre-

---

[98] Scott (1998).

Inclusive processes required for sustainable wellbeing

ative ideas are primarily generated bottom up, not top down, through interactions and cross-fertilisations of ideas promulgated by human contacts via various means. A critical role for the policymaker is that of connecting and supporting. Creativity remains the source of innovation, technological progress, and prosperity under all frameworks – how we encourage and support it is the point of difference. Think of a landscaper rather than an architect – the focus is on creating the right ecosystems for people, communities and ideas to flourish.

This type of policy framework embraces localism, encouragement of experimentation at the local level, small steps in implementation, reversibility and fast failures, and planning on surprises. It is built around the benefits of decentralisation and emergence. Collective wellbeing is pursued not by searching for investment levers that will enhance well-defined social outcomes, rather by making it easier for people to pursue the varied lives they value, with no predefined desired social outcomes.

As Beinhocker (2016) argues, we must take a more deliberately evolutionary view of policy development. Rather than thinking of policy as a fixed set of rules or institutions engineered to address a specific set of issues, we should think of policy as an adapting portfolio of experiments that helps shape the evolution of the economy and society over time.

There are three principles underpinning this approach:

- Rather than predict, we should encourage experimentation in communities and at local levels, and then supporting local experiments, aimed at addressing local problems, when they are having locally desired outcomes. It is wise to undertake these experiments on a small scale first, ascertain which work, scale-up the ones that are working, and eliminate the ones that are not. Such an evolutionary approach recognises the complexity of social-economic systems, the difficulty of predicting what solutions will work in advance, and difficulties in real-world implementation. Failures then happen on a small scale and become opportunities to learn rather than hard-to-reverse policy disasters.

💙 Policies and institutions should be made as adaptable as possible. A good approach is to create rules that provide general frameworks, but then adapt to specific circumstances. One example is the way that California's building codes have succeeded in reducing energy consumption. Rather than try to predict the state of energy-efficient technologies in future years, the regulators created a set of general performance standards that automatically ratchet up as the state of technology improved.

💙 And finally, policy makers need to think of themselves less as social engineers and more as system stewards. As Michael Hallsworth from the Institute for Government (IFG) explains, rather than engineering specific outcomes, government's role as system steward is to create the conditions in which interacting agents in the system will adapt towards socially desirable outcomes. Policy design and implementation are thought of as integral rather than separately, and mechanisms for feedback and continuous learning and improvement are built in from the beginning.[99]

Institutions and wellbeing

In a complex and evolving world dominated by radical uncertainty, the scope and instruments of public policy available to a wellbeing state need to be expanded to include the comprehensive

---

[99] See Beinhocker (2016), from where this material is sourced, for a more detailed discussion of all these points.

ecosystem that surrounds all decision makers. Instead of using direct interventions to achieve certain goals, the government could rather try to influence the rules of the game. The rules of the game are the institutions that define the individual agents' action sets.

In this context, North (1994) describes institutions as 'the humanly devised constraints that structure human interaction. They are made up of formal constraints (rules, laws, constitutions), informal constraints (norms of behaviour, conventions, and self-imposed codes of conduct), and their enforcement characteristics. Together they define the incentive structure of societies and specifically economies.'[100]

Hodgson (2006) offers a broader definition of institutions as systems of established and embedded social rules that structure social interactions. Institutions do not just constrain and influence the choices and actions of individual consumers and businesses. They also perform a critical enabling function, and their evolution is endogenous.[101]

According to North (1990, 1991), institutions comprise both informal constraints (such as sanctions, taboos, customs, traditions, codes of conduct) and formal rules (such as constitutions, laws, property rights). The former form part of the heritage we refer to as culture, while the latter are created by the state. In both cases, their fundamental role is to create order and reduce uncertainty.[102]

When wider wellbeing is the objective of public policy, what types of institutions are most suited, as instruments, to delivering that objective? Bennett et al. (2016) trace the origins of this

---

[100] p2.
[101] Arvanitidis (2004), Acemoglu and Robinson (2013).
[102] Bennett et al. (2016), p7.

exploration to the classical economists Adam Smith, John Stuart Mill, and David Ricardo, stating that they 'stressed the importance of institutions, public policy, and the rule of law in shaping economic performance and human wellbeing'.[103]

The modern version of this line of exploration, under the themes fundamental (as distinct from proximate) causes of economic growth and development and deep roots of economic development, is well represented by the works of Acemoglu and Robinson (2013) and Spolaore and Wacziarg (2013), among many others.[104]

Case for localism as an institution

Rajan (2019) describes localism as 'the process of decentralising power to the local level so that people feel more empowered in their communities. The community, rather than the nation, will become a possible vehicle for ethnic cohesiveness and cultural continuity.' The underlying principle is that of *subsidiarity*: 'powers should stay at the most decentralised level consistent with their effective use'.[105]

This does not mean that community powers will be unchecked. 'The state will have the responsibility of creating an inclusive framework at the national level, using open-access markets to include and connect a diverse set of local communities.' Communities will be open to goods and services from across the nation, and the free flow of people, both in and out, will be guaranteed by law. This will all be assisted by free and competitive markets, and technology.[106]

---

[103] pp5–6.

[104] See also Hodgson (2014) for a broader discussion of institutions in the context of evolutionary economics. *Appendix 1* in this book provides a brief survey of the empirical literature on the effects of institutions on economic and social outcomes.

[105] p285.

[106] Ibid. p285.

| Inclusive processes required for sustainable wellbeing

Figure 13. Weaving our connections and contributions

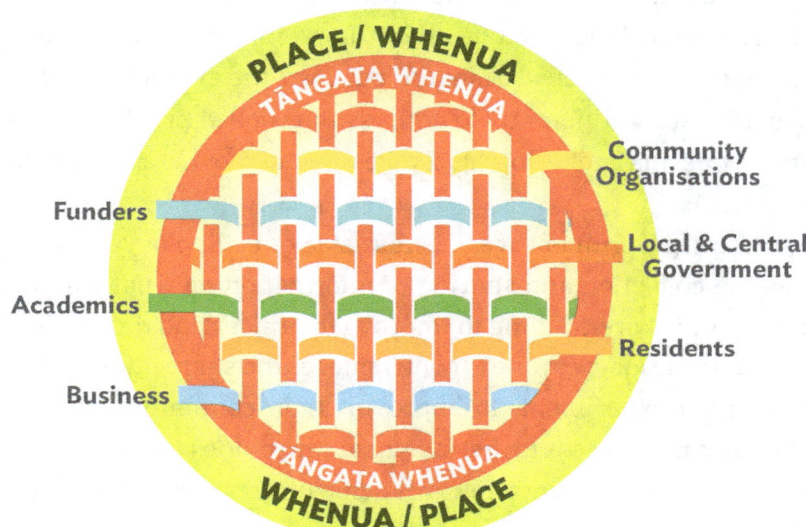

Te Whakawhanake ā-Hapori
Weaving our connections and contributions

In the New Zealand context, the spirit of localism is very nicely captured by figure 13, which I have borrowed from Inspiring Communities (2020).

The figure highlights the recognition that 'successful solutions cannot be parachuted in from the outside. Success is framed within a collective lens – a local systems approach – where everyone has something to contribute to activate positive change.'[107]

In a country where different communities, cities and regions are prospering, potentially in very different ways, people have far wider opportunities to live the kinds of lives they want to live, without leaving the country.

---

[107] Inspiring Communities (2020), p2.

The role of good governance (see chapter 5) is to create the environment where such collaboration is encouraged and takes place. This includes, among other interventions, the communication of a strong sense of shared purpose, the empowerment of people to work differently to address the wicked problems they are addressing and to do what it takes, and to provide appropriate resourcing.[108]

Central government agencies, assisted by technology that enables the collection and sharing of information on what various communities are trialling to improve their lives could provide a live database for everyone to contribute to, and share information about their experiments in improving their communities' lives. They also have access to the analytical capabilities to assess what works and what does not, towards achieving community-defined objectives, to aid with investment decisions.

If there is to be increased devolved responsibility to local and regional governments for the delivery of services, this needs to be accompanied by increased sources of funding – with associated strong controls and incentives. As Crampton and Acharya (2015) argue, regional and local councils should be given a share of additional tax revenues generated when economic growth-enhancing policies are successfully implemented in the regions.

Several scholars, including Hayek (2013), note that the fundamental case for localism – deliberately supporting the flourishing of local communities and economies – is that local government is closer to the people it serves, is better able to reflect the needs of communities, is critical for the health and vitality of democracy, and provides a greater variety of choice that can accommodate different valued lives.

In this context, it is interesting and important to note the fol-

---

[108] Inspiring Communities (2020), p7.

lowing words from the Municipal Corporations Act 1842 in New Zealand:

> '...the inhabitants themselves are best qualified, as well as by their more intimate knowledge of local affairs, as by their direct interests therein, to provide for the wants and needs of their respective settlements. ... the central government would thus be deprived of the power of partiality in its legislation; while at the same time, the prosperity of the country at large, would be promoted by the honourable rivalry which would spring up among the various settlements.'

The rationale behind localism also finds support in the literature on incomplete contracts. The basic idea is to focus on the allocation of residual decision rights through ownership decisions, as the fundamental response to uncertainty and contractual incompleteness. The ability to exercise residual control rights increases incentives to make relationship-specific investments by improving the ex-post bargaining position of an asset owner. Asset ownership should therefore be assigned to those with the potential to make the most important (value-enhancing), relationship-specific investments.

For example, the importance of the relationship between general practitioners (GPs) and their patients provides an explanation for the fact that GPs are the part of the health sector that in almost every country is privatised (that is, GPs, not the government, 'own' the relationship with the patient). This leads to the recommendation that there should be less central government ownership of service delivery, with wider delegation of responsibility for investment in outcomes and customer relationships to private or community service delivery organisations.[109]

---

[109] Evans, Quigley, Guthrie (2012).

In general, communities and regions want to own and solve their own problems; they are keen to pursue a partnership model with the central government. They want central government to facilitate, and participate in, exploratory conversations around the respective roles and responsibilities of central and local government in promoting regional economic development and broader wellbeing. They are keen on mutually respecting and beneficial *partnerships*.

One of the skills communities do not have, for example, is setting up controlled trials and then evaluating their performance. Nor do they have the knowhow, technology and resources, to collect and share the data gathered from these trials so that they contribute to broader learning.

Localism – not a panacea

Localism, while a critical ingredient of public governance in addressing wicked problems, is not a panacea. Nothing is.

One of the key issues relates to the collective action problem.[110] In essence, the problem, as it relates to managing the natural environment (just to take one example), can be described as follows. Power of private interests is concentrated, organised and effective. Public interest, on the other hand, relies on a diffuse collective concerned with environmental damage. Benefits gained from extraction are much greater than any loss incurred at an individual level. Everyone gains benefits from nature, but not enough obvious benefits to fight as hard as those that benefit from extraction. No one feels the losses as hard either from environmental damage. So the odds tend to be in the favour of the damaging actions over conservation. The adverse consequences of this specific problem for natural resource management in gen-

---

[110] Olson (1971).

eral, and fresh water management in particular, in New Zealand are extremely well analysed by Brown (2017).

This provides one plausible explanation as to why localism, despite being promoted as a great idea for a very long time, has not been embraced and implemented with enthusiasm in New Zealand.

At an international level, another main determinant of the degree of localism in various countries is the level of *trust* in local versus central government. One example comes from Sweden. After endorsing the view that there are good reasons to expect that citizens will appreciate local government more than central government, Erlingsson (2020) goes on to explain why, over the last few years, Swedes have started to trust municipalities less than the central government:

> '...the unfortunate combination of three factors have brought about this curious circumstance: 1) the far-reaching decentralisation and principal role Swedish municipalities have successively been given in implementing assignments which lie at the heart of Swedish welfare state policies; 2) that several of the municipalities' assignments are particularly susceptible to corruption; and 3) that the increase in responsibilities as well as the increased danger zones for corruption has not been accompanied by institutions that ensure transparency and checks-and-balances in local government, ultimately leaving Swedish local government with institutions that obfuscate accountability.'[111]

Institutions are an incomplete prescription for sustained wellbeing
Good institutions are a critical, and necessary, foundation for an

---

[111] p1.

effective wellbeing policy. There is a huge volume of literature, supported by heaps of empirical evidence, that good institutions are necessary – in fact critical – for sustainably good environmental, social and economic outcomes.

But are they adequate? Amartya Sen (2017)[112] distinguishes between two traditions:

Social contract tradition
- Nature of the perfectly just society – perfection-focused approach.
- Institution-focused – concentrating on getting the institutions right.

Social choice approach
This approach focuses on social realisations, including:

- Outcomes that emerge, as well as ...
- ... the processes through which those outcomes come about.

The focus here is on comparative justice and injustice, concentrating on actual outcomes that reflect not only institutions but also social interactions and other factors that generate actual outcomes.

What matters is not only getting the institutions right, but also what results from these institutions and other arrangements – reflecting actual behaviours and social interactions – dealing with and removing manifest injustices.

This is also precisely the point made by Banerjee and Duflo (2011) as well when they critically but constructively analyse the effectiveness of macro institutions in improving people's lives,

---

[112] pp362–364.

Inclusive processes required for sustainable wellbeing

also citing other scholars such as William Easterly and Jeffrey Sachs. 'The focus on broad INSTITUTIONS as a necessary and sufficient condition for anything good to happen is somewhat misplaced.'[113]

As a complement, they advocate a ground-up (organic) approach to the emergence of good institutions, gradually over time, suited to local circumstances and needs, and supported by central governments as appropriate. Such institutions cannot be imported and/or imposed from abroad. They need to be nourished from within, supported by freedom and liberty.

> 'Careful understanding of the motivations and constraints of everyone (poor people, civil servants, taxpayers, elected politicians, and so on) can lead to policies and institutions that are better designed, and less likely to be perverted by corruption or dereliction of duty. These changes will be incremental, but they will sustain and build on themselves. They can be the start of a quiet revolution.'[114]

Critical role of political economy

This all fits in nicely with a very rich literature on complexity economics, institutional economics, and evolutionary economics, which are totally in tune with the Darwinian theory of evolution – arguing that a deliberate policy of encouraging different local experiments, and then selecting and amplifying the successful ones, can help complex economic and social systems evolve and flourish. The distinctive role of policy is to encourage, nudge, and support, while putting controls in place to prevent the building of excesses.[115]

---

[113] p264.
[114] p265.
[115] See Arthur (2014), Ostrom (2009).

As Dietz *et al.* (2003) put it, 'Human institutions – ways of organising activities – affect the resilience of the environment. Locally evolved institutional arrangements governed by stable communities and buffered from outside forces have sustained resources successfully for centuries, although they often fail when rapid change occurs. Ideal conditions for governance are increasingly rare. Critical problems, such as transboundary pollution, tropical deforestation, and climate change, are at larger scales and involve nonlocal influences. Promising strategies for addressing these problems include dialogue among interested parties, officials, and scientists; complex, redundant, and layered institutions; a mix of institutional types; and designs that facilitate experimentation, learning, and change.'[116]

However, this is where political economy challenges come into play.

> 'A major challenge for these more adaptive approaches to policy is the political difficulty of failure. Learning from a portfolio of experiments necessitates that some experiments will fail. Evolution is a highly innovative but inherently wasteful process – many options are often tried before the right one is discovered. Yet politicians are held to an impossibly high standard, where any failure, large or small, can be used to call into question their entire record.
>
> 'Likewise, politicians are always expected to have clear plans, and simple, easy to understand answers in which they have unshakeable confidence. You would never hear a politician give a speech where she or he says, "It is a complex problem, we're not sure what to do. But we have several good ideas that we'll try on a small scale. We'll then ramp up the ones that

---
[116] p1907.

Inclusive processes required for sustainable wellbeing

work and close down the ones that don't, and then have a good shot at solving it."

'For some reason, we don't mind such an approach when it is used by doctors looking for new drugs, energy companies looking for oil, or venture capitalists looking for the next big idea. But we seem to prefer politicians who tell us the world is simple and predictable, even though we know it to be complex and unpredictable.

'So, an explicit, widespread use of new economic approaches to policymaking may require some education of citizens, the media and politicians themselves on the risks of overconfident top-down solutions, and the importance of small-scale failures as a way to learn and prevent large-scale disasters.'[117]

7. How do we know if policy is effective?

There is now an emerging consensus on the need to augment income with complementary measures of wellbeing in evaluating the success of public policy, since income is not a good proxy for all indicators of wellbeing.

While dissatisfaction with income as a measure of wellbeing has a long history,[118] the move to expand measures of wellbeing beyond income was given a significant impetus with the publication of the report of the Stiglitz-Sen-Fitoussi Commission.[119] Useful surveys of this broad literature are provided by the contributions in Adler and Fleurbaey (2016).

At a practical level, and consistent with the point about the inadequacy of an exclusive or primary focus on income as a source or measure of wellbeing, we can assess whether we are pursuing and achieving genuinely wellbeing-focused policy objectives through four complementary lenses.

First, by establishing whether more resources are being made available to support better lives – say, more funding for housing.

Second, by assessing whether these resources are being converted into higher capabilities and opportunities (i.e. 'functionings') for a better life – say, better quantity and quality of housing.

---

[118] See, for example, Coyle (2014, 2015); Nordhaus and Tobin (1972); Saunders and Dalziel (2017); Waring (1988); Fleurbaey and Blanchet (2013); Boarini and d'Ercole (2013); van den Bergh (2009).

[119] Stiglitz *et al.* (2009).

| Love you – *Public policy for intergenerational wellbeing*

Figure 14. Wellbeing snapshot – current and future

New Zealand's current well-being, 2018 or latest available year

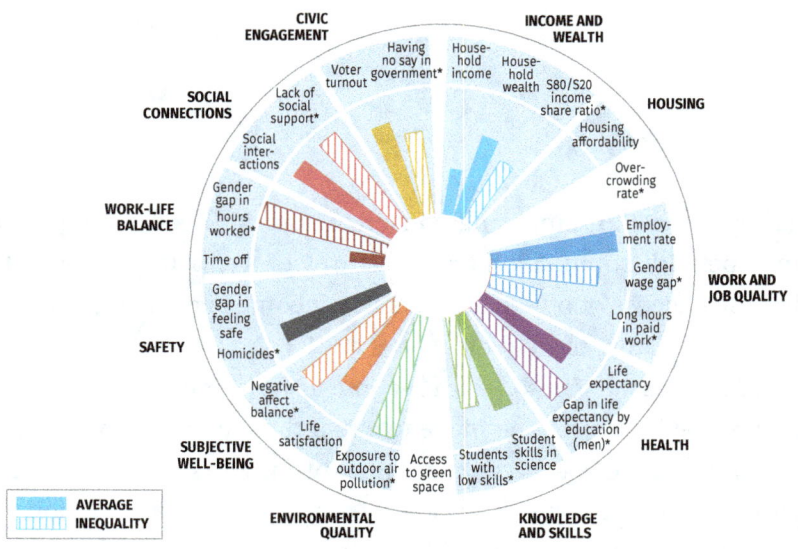

Note: This chart shows New Zealand's relative strengths and weaknesses in well-being compared to other OECD countries. Longer bars always indicate better outcomes (i.e. higher wellbeing), whereas shorter bars always indicate worse outcomes (lower well-being) – including for negative indicators, marked with an *, which have been reverse-scored. Inequalities (gaps between top and bottom, differences between groups, people falling under a deprivation threshold) are shaded with stripes, and missing data in white.

New Zealand's resources for future well-being, 2018 or latest available year

Natural Capital	Economic Capital	Human Capital	Social Capital
Greenhouse gas emissions per capita ❸ ↗	Produced fixed assets ❷ ↗	Educational attainment of young adults ❷ ↗	Trust in others ❶ …
Material footprint ❷ ↘	Financial net worth of government ❶ ↔	Premature mortality ❷ ↔	Trust in government ❶ ↔
Red List Index of threatened species ❸ ↘	Household debt ❷ ↔	Labour underutilisation rate ❷ ↗	Gender parity in politics ❷ ↔

Note: ❶=top-performing OECD tier, ❷=middle-performing OECD tier, ❸=bottom-performing OECD tier. ↗indicates consistent improvement; ↔ indicates no clear or consistent trend; ↘indicates consistent deterioration, and "…" indicates insufficient time series to determine trends since 2010. For methodological details, see the Reader's Guide of How's Life? 2020.

Third, and as a complementary step to the first two, by simply asking people, through various survey-based assessments of subjective wellbeing, whether their lives are improving or not. As a subset of, and complement to, this third tool, we can also specifically target the most disadvantaged people in the population and ask them whether their lives are improving.

Where intergenerational wellbeing is the objective of public policy, there needs to be a fourth assessment specifically targeted at evaluating whether public policy is creating the platform for sustainable intergenerational wellbeing. Good public policies, in this specific context, are those that enlarge the wellbeing garden. To anticipate what follows, this is an attempt to apply a rights based, as distinct from a utility centred, evaluative framework to public policy choices.[120]

When we are dealing with a multidimensional wellbeing function, policy makers will always be looking for policy interventions that have multiple and mutually reinforcing benefits. Below we assess New Zealand's progress on wellbeing through these complementary lenses.

Looking backward

Figure 14 is from OECD (2020 c). It provides a summary of current (top half) and future-looking (bottom half) indicators of wellbeing.

New Zealanders generally enjoy high levels of wellbeing, as indicated by the OECD's How's Life indicators. Overall, outcomes are particularly good for employment and long-term unemployment, housing size, perceived health, social support and air quality.

Compared with other OECD countries, average earnings and

---

[120] Sen (2017), p420.

household income are low, reflecting low productivity, housing affordability is a significant challenge, a large share of people usually work long hours (50 or more per week) or do not have much time off work, and feelings of safety are below the OECD average.

Over the last decade, child poverty rates have increased on some measures (such as those based on a relative poverty line of 50 percent of median equivalised disposable household income before housing costs) but declined on others (such as those based on the same relative poverty line but after housing costs).'[121]

We can also assess New Zealand's performance relative to its own history, for example by considering recent trends. As we can see from table 2 below, from the 2017 *OECD Review of New Zealand*,[122] some of the components of wellbeing – including income and wealth, the employment rate, real earnings, work-life balance, life expectancy at birth – have improved in New Zealand over the past ten years, while others – labour market insecurity, incidence of job strain, housing affordability, civic engagement – have deteriorated. Note that subjective wellbeing (SWB) is separately reported in table 2.

A very detailed analysis of SWB across various population segments, classified by gender, ethnicity, age etc., is provided by McLeod (2018). Beneath the bonnet of an on average high wellbeing picture for New Zealand, that work highlights a number of significant inequalities, which were also picked up in the *Wellbeing Budget 2019*.

By way of an example, figure 15 presents the wellbeing performance of our Maori population relative to New Zealand averages.

---

[121] OECD (2019 a), p7.
[122] OECD (2017 a).

How do we know if policy is effective?

Table 2. Change in New Zealand's average wellbeing over the past ten years

Dimension	Description	Change
Income and wealth	Household net adjusted disposable income has increased over the past decade. After rising sharply from 2005 to 2007, growth stalled in 2008, resuming in recent years and peaking in 2013.	↗
Jobs and earnings	In 2015, the employment rate was very close to its 2005 level, having fallen from 2006 to 2010 and gradually recovered in more recent years. Real earnings in New Zealand are 14% higher than a decade ago. Other job indicators have worsened in the last 10 years: labour market insecurity remains relatively high compared to 2005, and the incidence of job strain has risen by almost 7 percentage points.	↔ ↗ ↘ ↘
Housing conditions	The number of rooms per person has remained relatively stable since 2005, and above the OECD average. Housing affordability has meanwhile worsened slightly in the past decade, with the proportion of income spent on housing costs increasing from 25.8% in 2005 to 26.2% in 2014.	↔ ↘
Work-life balance	The share of employees working 50 hours or more per week fell by 2 percentage points from 2005 to 2015 in New Zealand, steeper than the 0.7 fall recorded for the OECD on average over the same period.	↗
Health status	Life expectancy at birth has improved by roughly 2 years since 2005, in line with the OECD average increase. Self-reported health has remained relatively stable from 2007 to 2016.	↗ ↔
Education and skills	The share of adults having completed upper secondary education increased by 2.5 percentage points from 2014 to 2016 (comparable data are not available prior to 2014).	↗
Social connections	The share of people who have relatives or friends whom they can count on to help in case of need has remained reasonably stable in the past 10 years.	↔
Civil engagement	Voter turnout among the population registered to vote fell by 3.3 percentage points between the 2005 and 2014 general elections.	↘
Environmental quality	Both satisfaction with local water quality and exposure to PM2.5 air pollution have remained relatively stable in New Zealand over the past decade.	↔ ↔
Personal security	The rate of deaths due to assault has fallen by almost one-quarter compared to 2005. The proportion of people who feel safe when walking alone at night has increased gradually, from 61% in 2005–2007 to 65% in 2014–16.	↗ ↗
Subjective wellbeing	Life satisfaction in New Zealand has remained broadly stable and at relatively high levels over the past decade.	↔

Note: for each indicator in every dimension: ↗ refers to an improvement; ↔ indicates little or no change; and ↘ signals deterioration. This is based on a comparison of the starting year (2005 in most cases) and the latest available year (usually 2015 or 2016). The order of the arrows shown in column three corresponds to that of the indicators mentioned in column two.

Source: OECD (2017 b). *How's Life?* – https://www.keepeek.com//Digital-Asset-Management/oecd/economics/how-s-life-2017_how_life-2017-en#.Wpu1EuhubD4

Figure 15. Māori wellbeing measures viz NZ averages

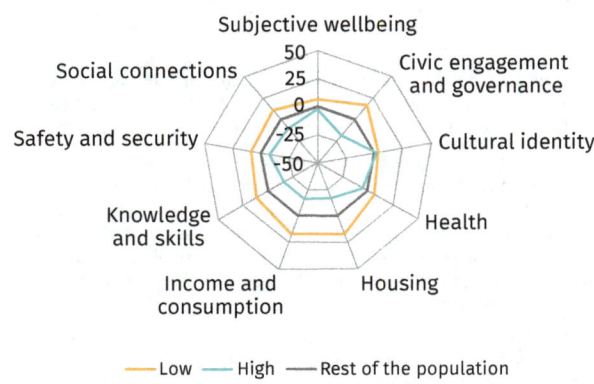

Looking forward

'New Zealand fares well in several aspects of the four capitals – natural, financial and physical, human, and social – that underpin future well-being. At least half of the indicators monitored by the OECD in each category rank amongst the top third of OECD countries, except for financial and physical capital.

'Nevertheless, reforms will be needed to counter the deterioration over the past decade in some areas of relative strength, notably students' cognitive skills at age 15, long-term unemployment and land area covered by forests.

'New Zealand does less well in building knowledge capital through R&D, natural capital through greenhouse gas (GHG) emissions and freshwater abstractions, and human capital owing to the spread of obesity. The expansion of dairy farming has catalysed a deterioration in water quality, and biodiversity is under threat.

'Social capital is particularly strong. A factor that contributes to [it] is low perceptions of corruption, although there has been

How do we know if policy is effective?

Figure 16. 'Genuine savings'

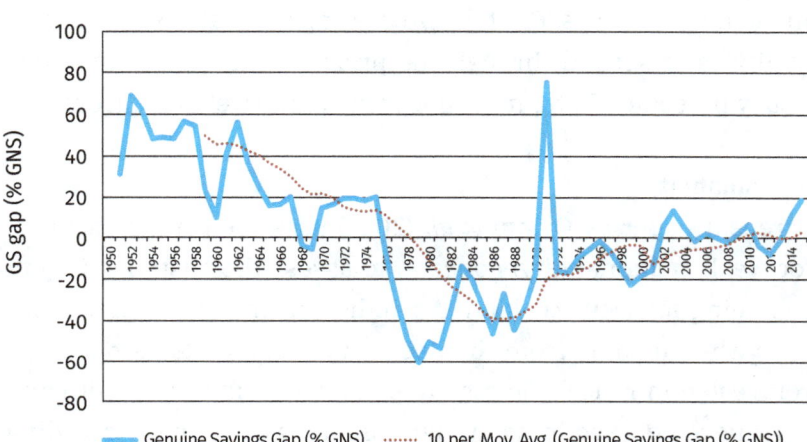

Positive (negative) number is **bad** (good) as it shows the country is saving **less** (more) than required to maintain sustainability.

some deterioration in recent years. Perceptions of the use of public power for private gain are also low.'[123]

In summarising, both the backward looking and current as well as future-looking indicators of wellbeing in New Zealand, the OECD Report (2019 a) states:

'Well-being is high on most dimensions but weaknesses, such as relatively low productivity and earnings, uneven distribution, challenges of housing affordability and child well-being, and threats to natural capital, need to be addressed.

'Embedding the well-being approach further into public policymaking holds the promise of making policy advice and implementation more effective, through better targeted actions, a deeper understanding of trade-offs, and more coordinated collaboration across agencies.'[124]

---

[123] OECD (2019 a), p7.
[124] OECD (2019 a), p11.

The future-looking summary presented above can be complemented in two ways. First, by presenting an analysis of 'sustainability', and second through the prism of the quality of public policy presented in figure 4, the prism of the wellbeing frontier.

Sustainability

A recent paper by Qasim *et al.* (2018) uses the genuine savings (or weak sustainability) concept, to assess the sustainability of wellbeing for New Zealand. An indicator of weak sustainability is when income from the use of non-renewable resources is reinvested in renewable resources to maintain total wealth and to achieve non-declining human wellbeing over time. According to this framework, an economy which saves more than the combined depreciation of its stocks of natural capital and produced capital will be weakly sustainable.[125]

Although Qasim *et al.* (2018) report some evidence of weak sustainability for the New Zealand economy over the long term (1950–2015), they also report on indicators highlighting pressures arising from strong population growth and low productivity growth on the sustainability of wellbeing in New Zealand.

As a nation, New Zealand is not saving sufficiently to expect growing wellbeing over time. Figure 16 demonstrates this result in the form of a gross savings gap expressed as a percentage of gross national savings. The gap measures the extent to which New Zealand as a nation needs to increase its saving in order to maintain its per capita wellbeing over time. The key message is that New Zealand should continue to increase its savings and investing at levels necessary to ensure sustainable future increases in wellbeing.

---

[125] Ibid, p2.

| How do we know if policy is effective?

Wellbeing garden

I start by providing some measures that shed light on recent trends in the key pillars defining the boundaries of the wellbeing garden, before I then present the evolution of the size and shape of the garden across time. This is my attempt to operationalise the assessment of the success or failure of an intergenerational rights-based evaluative framework for public policy.[126]

The OECD's (2017, 2019) assessments of trends in New Zealand, when viewed through the lens of the main pillars defining the boundaries of the wellbeing garden, highlight some of the stresses building on the shape and size of the garden:

- On *equity*, 'Disposable income inequality is above the OECD average, reflecting less-than-average redistribution through taxes and transfers ... and the child-poverty rate, which is around the OECD average, is more than double the rate in the best performing OECD countries. Living standards and economic growth also vary considerably ethnically and geographically.'[127]

  'House prices have risen, affordability has dropped and homelessness is high, calling for urgent reforms to ease constraints on housing supply.'[128]

- A recent paper by Smith (2018) has also raised serious concerns about poverty in New Zealand, emphasising the point that, improving economic indicators such as the declining unemployment rate, has not been able to reverse the trend of increasing poverty in the country.

- With respect to the *potential economic growth rate*, productivity

---

[126] Sen (2017), p420.
[127] OECD (2017 a), p16.
[128] OECD (2019 a), p12.

is highlighted in both the 2017 and 2019 reports as a challenge. This is a major influence on the potential growth rate of the economy. 'Despite generally good macroeconomic- and structural policy settings, New Zealand has relatively low productivity levels and hence earnings.'[129]

- On matters relating to *environmental quality*, the OECD report (2017 a) notes that: [These same messages are again emphasised in the OECD (2019 a) Review.]

  - Strong growth in primary industries may jeopardise environmental quality. Pollution from farming and urbanisation is reducing water quality, and water scarcity is an increasing concern.
  - Greenhouse gas emissions are high and continue to grow. While half of emissions come from agriculture, total transport and industry emissions are rising fastest.
  - New Zealand has one of the world's largest shares of threatened species. (*Executive summary*).

- On social capital, which provides the foundation for *social cohesion*, the OECD (2019 a) is complimentary on New Zealand's performance: 'Social capital is particularly strong. A factor that contributes to high social capital is low perceptions of corruption, although there has been some deterioration in recent years. Perceptions of the use of public power for private gain are also low.'[130]

We can complement the preceding analysis with a measure of the evolution of the size and shape of the wellbeing garden. In this context, figure 17 should be seen as illustrative only, since the underlying data is pretty weak. We do not have consistent

---

[129] OECD (2019 a), p12.
[130] p7.

How do we know if policy is effective?

Figure 17. Evolution of the New Zealand wellbeing garden (or frontier)

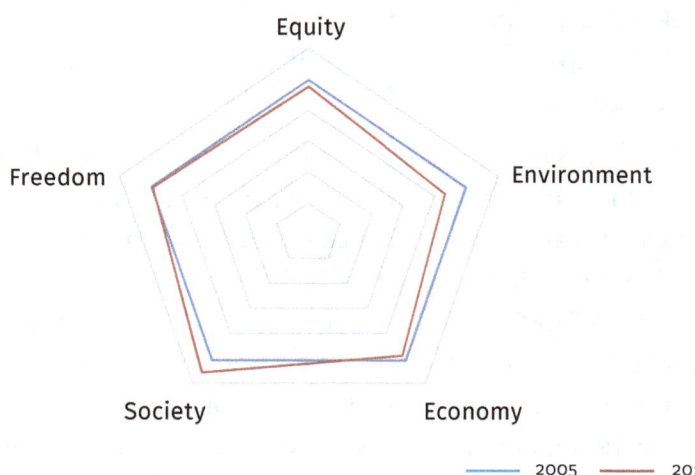

data over a long period of time to provide a basis for reliable time series on the five pillars that define the boundary of the garden. This is why we have deliberately provided only two representations of the perimeter of the garden, based on data for (around) the periods 2005 and 2018. Treating 2005 as the base (index no = 100), we have represented the 2018 data as a deviation (ratio) of the same (or corresponding) measure from that base.

If we wish to assess public policy from an intergenerational wellbeing perspective, we need high-quality data to help us measure the size of the wellbeing garden. In the words attributed to Antoine de Saint-Exupery, 'If you want to build a ship, don't drum up people to collect wood and don't assign them tasks and work, but rather teach them to long for the endless immensity of the sea.'[131]

♥ The *equity* dimension of the wellbeing frontier conceptually

---

[131] https://bobramseyseminars.com/2014/04/15/if-you-want-to-build-a-ship

represents widespread access to all forms of wealth. We have used the data presented in one of the reports to the Tax Working Group[132] on wealth inequality, using a wealth Gini coefficient as a measure.

- The *Environmental Quality* measure is from Wendling *et al.* (2018) based on their *Environmental Performance Index*. The index covers 24 performance indicators across 10 'issue categories' covering environmental health and ecosystem vitality. New Zealand's ranking went from 1 to 17 between 2006 and 2018 – and its performance index went from 88.0 to 76.0. However, the authors warn that because of changes in index-construction methodology, this comparison may be misleading. Based on a baseline score of 73 (roughly based on ten years ago), one can see the score of 76 as an improvement. In short, like with the other data used to construct the wellbeing frontiers between 2005 (or thereabouts) and 2018 (or thereabouts), these data need to be viewed with caution.

- The *economy* represents the potential growth rate of the economy – and is sourced from the OECD Databases (*OECD Data*; *OECD Statistics*).

- The *society* dimension conceptually represents *social cohesion* and is proxied by survey-based generalised trust data, obtained from Ospina and Rozer (2016).

- The *freedom* measure is based on the *Human Freedom Index* constructed by Vásquez and Porčnik (2019).

Broadly speaking, based on the evidence and data presented in this section, we can conclude that there are stresses building on New Zealand's wellbeing garden. These stresses are concen-

---

[132] IRD and NZ Treasury (2018).

trated on the natural environment and equity. If these stresses are not addressed, they have the potential to create pressure on social cohesion and potential economic growth as well. These are the main sources of concern about the strength of the platform for an intergenerationally sustainable wellbeing for New Zealand.

As the OECD (2019 a) *Review* summarises: 'Well-being is high on most dimensions but weaknesses, such as relatively low productivity and earnings, uneven distribution, challenges of housing affordability and child well-being, and threats to natural capital, need to be addressed.'[133]

If required for policy analysis and prioritisation,[134] the total 'size' of the wellbeing garden (WG) can be calculated by multiplying the measures for each of the five domains: WG = Eq x En x Ec x So x Fr. Viable policy interventions – those that push out or leave unmoved each of the five pillars defining the boundaries of the wellbeing garden – can then be prioritised by ranking their impact on the ratio of the change in the size of the garden, thus measured, to the cost of the intervention (some sort of benefit/cost analysis). We would do this in comparing only viable policy interventions.

Doing so could be subject to the same types of criticism that the well-known equation I = P x A x T has been subjected to. The expression equates human impact on the environment (I) to the product of three factors: population (P), affluence (A), and technology (T). One of these criticisms is that the equation ignores (or makes light of) the interdependencies between P, A, T – and implicitly treats them as independent.[135]

Such interdependencies are at the centre of our modelling work (see Karacaoglu *et al.* 2019 and chapter 9 of this book). They

---

[133] p11.
[134] See chapter 8 of this book.
[135] Chertow (2008), Wikipedia I=PAT.

help us prioritise potential policy interventions aimed at expanding the wellbeing garden. The suggested measure of the size of the garden is simply a proxy for the failure or success of such policy interventions. This is what I turn to in the next chapter.

Before I do so, it is worth emphasising that there are other evaluative frameworks, which can be viewed as complementary to, and narrower than, the one suggested here. Among such alternatives, the prominent one is based on measures of subjective wellbeing (SWB), and variations thereof (such as equivalent incomes). These are essentially variations of what Sen (2017, p420) refers to as 'utility-centred' evaluative frameworks. A practical application and illustration is provided by cost-benefit analyses of projects, where the measurement of both costs and benefits is in terms of subjective wellbeing (or equivalent incomes) – cost-wellbeing analyses.[136] These are perfectly suitable for small-world exercises (to use the language of Kay and King 2020), such as cost-benefit analyses of projects, in environments of limited uncertainty.

Our focus is on the design and implementation of public policy at a system level, as it relates to the large world (of Kay and King 2020) – and one that is dominated by radical uncertainty. We suggest that in that type of social choice environment, our complementary approach adds distinctive value, especially when we are assessing the comparative merits of longer-term systemic interventions, focused on enhancing intergenerational wellbeing. We suggest that using the categorisation proposed by Sen (2017, p420) this would represent a rights-based policy approach – where the expansion of the wellbeing garden symbolises enhanced opportunities for all concerned, including future generations, to live the lives they value.

---

[136] Adler and Fleurbaey (2016), Frijters *et al.* (2019), Jara and Schokkaert (2016), MacCulloch (2016) provide examples and lots of references.

8. What would I prioritise and why?

If there were the political will to set up the governance and funding structures along the lines advocated in chapter 5, then the processes outlined in that chapter would generate the required prioritisation through a very inclusive process. Such prioritisation needs to be informed by analysis and evidence.

If I were advising an Independent Office of Wellbeing (IOW) in New Zealand on what we need to be prioritising, given where we are right now as a country, what would my advice be – towards laying the foundation for a better future and why?

Prioritisation

Martin and Pindyck (2015) pose the following question: faced with numerous potential catastrophes, with uncertainties surrounding occurrences and timings, which should society attempt to avert? Of course, we can also ask the question in a positive way: faced with numerous investment opportunities at a systems level, which should society prioritise? In answering this question, we need to keep in mind the policy objective of improving wellbeing on a sustainable basis across generations.

This is also the type of question on which the broader policy-oriented literature on the United Nations Sustainable Development Goals (SDGs) is increasingly focused:[137] considering the

---

[137] Griggs *et al.* (2013).

strong dependencies between these goals, which should we prioritise so that we achieve the highest sustainable social return on our investment? In planning for and prioritising these investments, it is critical that we take their complementarities in generating wellbeing into account.

Burns and Howard (2018) discuss the implications of the SDGs' multidimensional framework, arguing for a more integrated understanding of how the component dimensions interrelate. They argue that while it is possible to effect positive change in one dimension of wellbeing, there may be no practical improvement in an individual's circumstances unless there are parallel changes in related dimensions.[138]

In line with this broad literature, the answer suggested by our analysis is that priorities should be set by identifying policy interventions that have multiple, mutually reinforcing, benefits in terms of enhancing intergenerational wellbeing.

In principle, prioritisation of a set of viable policies when intergenerational wellbeing is the policy objective can be based on the change in the size of the wellbeing garden, subject to the constraint that viable policy interventions are those that push out or leave unmoved each of the five pillars surrounding the wellbeing garden.

Following the identification of the set of viable policy interventions, we would rank policies to reflect the ordering of the ratios of the expansion of the size of the frontier to the cost of the proposed intervention – a form of benefit-cost analysis, using a rights-based evaluative framework.

At this stage of the development of the wellbeing framework, we do not have adequate data nor a complete model, to apply such a thorough benefit-cost analysis for policy prioritisation. Nevertheless, what follows is based on the same principles.

---

[138] See also Burns and Worsley (2015), Clark (2005), Costanza *et al.* (2017).

| What would I prioritise and why?

My priorities
The priorities identified and discussed below have been informed by the stresses on the wellbeing frontier that were identified in chapter 7. These stresses are concentrated on the natural environment and equity. If they are not attended to with some degree of urgency, they will also start putting pressure on the other key dimensions of the wellbeing frontier, such as social cohesion. On the flip side, if they are dealt with adequately and in the right manner, they will have positive benefits for the other dimensions of wellbeing, such as potential economic growth.

The priorities and the way they are configured and applied also reflect the complementarities between the domains of wellbeing. These are arrived at through modelling exercises.

Top two priorities
Our own work[139] suggests that, given where we are right now, the top two priorities of a public policy that has intergenerational wellbeing as its primary objective, should be a universal and comprehensive leave no one behind strategy, complemented by investments that build resilience to systemic risks to the natural environment, both accompanied by just and viable transition strategies.

It is important to emphasise that this prioritisation is conditioned by our starting point, which includes (by way of examples) financial system stability and resilience, as well as social cohesion. In other words, at this stage, there are no apparent major stresses on these specific dimensions of the wellbeing garden.

Of course, the obvious next questions are: *why* (what is the justification for this specific set of prioritisations) and *how* (how would we give effect to them)?

---
[139] Karacaoglu *et al.* (2019).

Leaving no one behind

Let us start by emphasising that there is a huge difference between a leaving no one behind strategy and an anti-poverty strategy. The latter is primarily about reducing pain and deprivation today. It is about giving, redistribution and welfare. The former is about making sure that all citizens have the opportunities and capabilities (that is, substantial freedoms) to pursue the lives they value. It is about investing, enabling, pre-distribution and wellbeing.

These are of course complementary strategies, and they are all necessary. Nevertheless, 'Defining people by their problems is turning circumstance into essence. It denies hope.'[140] Camfield (2006) describes the advantages of a capabilities-based wellbeing approach from an ethnographic perspective. It spurs much needed critical awareness on the positive dimensions of the human experience, enabling researchers to explore what 'people have and are able to do, rather than focusing on their deficits, which should produce more credible and respectful representations of people's lives to inform development policy and practice.'[141]

Giving top priority to a leave no one behind strategy would make a positive contribution to all five dimensions of systemic resilience that we identified as critical in chapter 4. To see why this is so intuitively, imagine that we are all stakeholders in a private company. We may be workers in the company, or holding management positions in it, and/or shareholders, or may have lent the company funds.

Let us assume further that this company has demonstrated that it cares deeply about its employees. It has established a creche for the children of its employees. It has a hospital and medi-

---

[140] Banerjee and Duflo (2019), p322.
[141] Camfield (2006), p2.

cal centre that looks after them when they are unwell. It also has a retirement home where employees can live after their retirement, should they choose to do so. Workers and managers have an effective voice at the company Board table, through membership or other forms of representation.

As stakeholders we would be truly invested in this company. We would deeply care about its performance and sustainability. We would want it to do well. We would do our best to support it because when the company does well, we also do well, whatever stage of life we are in.

That is precisely what we wish to achieve with all our citizens. We want every citizen to be a stakeholder in the country in which we live. We want them to be invested in it. We want every citizen to be intensely interested in how the country is feeling and do their best for the wellbeing of the country at large, because when the country is doing well, each of us does well.

In such a country, each citizen would be intensely interested in how the government at all levels is performing, the quality of the natural environment, living at peace with each other, the country's economic performance – because there is something in the country' success for them, as individuals, as families, and as communities.

As Crouch (2020) expresses it:

'Democracy thrives when there are major opportunities for the mass of ordinary people to participate, through discussion and autonomous organizations, in shaping the agenda of public life, and when they are actively using these opportunities. ...

'Societies probably come closest to democracy in my maximal sense in the early years of achieving it or after great regime crises, when enthusiasm for democracy is widespread and concern for political developments intense, as people feel their lives are being touched by them; when many diverse groups and organizations of ordinary people share in the task of trying to frame a political agenda that will at last respond to their concerns; when the powerful interests that dominate undemocratic societies are wrong-footed and thrown on the defensive; and when the political system has not quite discovered how to manage and manipulate the new demands. These are democratic moments.'[142]

Broadening the availability of such opportunities and capabilities helps reduce inequity and increase social cohesion. Through that channel, it increases potential economic growth, as well as increasing social and economic resilience. It also directly reduces environmental degradation and increases environmental resilience because poverty is one of the biggest enemies of the environment.

'Many current social problems are rooted in our neglect of the democratic process. The solution isn't to dribble out enough crumbs to keep people at home, distracted, and otherwise pacified. Rather, we need to rejuvenate democratic politics, boost civic involvement, and seek collective solutions. Only with a mobilized, politically active society can we build the institutions we need for shared prosperity in the future, while protecting the most disadvantaged among us.'[143]

Investing towards a clean environment

An effective leaving no one behind strategy will have both posi-

---

[142] pp4–5.
[143] Acemoglu (2019).

tive and negative effects on the natural environment. As individuals' material, physical and psychological conditions improve, they tend to consume more. If nothing else is done, this higher consumption would lead to more pollution. On the other hand, people with higher incomes can afford to consume more environmentally friendly products, such as electric vehicles.

It follows that if we were able to complement a leave no one behind strategy with a set of public policies that encourage the production and consumption of cleaner products, we would concurrently be enhancing social, environmental, and economic resilience. This also provides an opportunity to direct any training and skilling programmes towards capabilities to operate cleaner technologies – contributing to both a leave no one behind strategy, as well as a cleaner environment strategy.

Just and viable transitions

All change is costly, and for some unsettling. In most cases of change, especially when major changes are involved, there will be winners and losers. On grounds of fairness, as well as maintaining equity and social cohesion during periods of change, it is critical that transitions are managed well and equitably. This is what just transitions are all about, and it takes us back to the critical importance of partnerships and mutual trust in designing and implementing wellbeing policies.

To take an example, based say on the efforts to move the Taranaki energy sector away from fossil fuels, if (as we do now) we wish to gradually adopt more environmentally friendly processes in our fuel production, current producers of these products need to be fully involved in every stage of the change process. No one goes out of their way to deliberately cause damage to the environment. It is all about working collaboratively, in the spirit of true partnership, to agree on where we want to get to and to manage the transition in a fair and equitable manner.

Focus on just transitions is very understandable and justifiable. It partly reflects the legacy of the immense transition harms that were inflicted on various communities by the economic policies of the 1980s and 1990s with their primary focus on economic efficiency.[144] Equally important for sustainable wellbeing, however, is the requirement of a complementary focus on viable transitions. As shown in Karacaoglu *et al.* (2019), viability theory is focused on ensuring that dynamic systems do not violate critical boundaries as they respond to policy changes or external shocks.

Viable policies are those that are chosen, designed and implemented in a way that ensures that critical environmental, social and economic boundaries are not crossed. In the context of intergenerational wellbeing, we define that critical boundary as the perimeter of the wellbeing garden of figure 4. As I pointed out in chapter 5, the works of Krumdieck (2020) and Transition-HQ are examples in New Zealand of efforts to make this idea practical. The wisdom that emanates from their explorations is that this cannot be centrally controlled – it needs to be embedded in the way we approach all our investment decisions, private and public. In this context, the fact that the four wellbeings framework is now adopted by local and regional governments in New Zealand, as well as the increasing focus of the corporate sector on multiple bottom lines, are very encouraging developments. The government should also insist on the New Zealand Infrastructure Commission adopting this viability framework in its selection and prioritisation of all infrastructure projects.

---

[144] See, for example, Evans *et al.* (1996).

What would I prioritise and why?

How will these priorities be achieved?
This sounds fantastic, but how do we propose to achieve all this?

First and foremost, there is a requirement that those in leadership positions develop and repeatedly communicate this narrative to the citizens. The core message of the narrative is that the combination of leaving no one behind and clean environment strategies would provide extremely high returns in terms of sustainable wellbeing, for ourselves as well as future generations.

The underlying narrative needs to be extremely well communicated and widely accepted if there is to be any chance of it being tried – let alone tried for long enough to work. We are talking about a massive transformational change in the way we govern this country which will require a commitment across several generations. This will not be achieved unless we have a shared narrative.

Although I did explain how this sort of massive transformation can be governed and funded in chapter 5, unless the broader narrative is widely endorsed and accountabilities for delivering the targeted wellbeing returns from these investments are clearly established and governed, there will be a huge amount of resentment about the financial costs associated with this transformation programme.

Second, by showing that we care. This means providing everyone with an opportunity to become a stakeholder in our society. By giving everyone access to education, healthcare and housing. By giving everyone who is capable, an employment opportunity. By making sure that everyone has a minimum level of adequate income. By looking after those who cannot look after themselves. By making sure that everyone has a voice in matters that affect them.

This is the essence of the idea behind *Universal Basic Services*,[145] as distinct from *Universal Basic Income*. One of the most contentious aspects of the conversations surrounding these ideas is whether these concepts are to be universal or means-tested. My strong preference is for means-tested access to government-provided and/or funded access to these primary services.

As Rajan (2020) puts it, 'Inequality is a real problem today, but it is the inequality of opportunity, of access to capabilities, of place, not just of incomes and wealth. Higher spending and thus taxes may be necessary, not to punish the rich but to help the left-behind find new opportunity. This requires fresh policies not discredited old ones.'

These policies need to be concurrently focused on reducing suffering, while increasing opportunities and capabilities to pursue valued lives.

For the current adult population, this needs to be delivered through training and employment opportunities as the top priority, and conditional cash support if the employment option is not available. Care also involves in-kind support as required for health and housing. For the young generation, the most effective and enduring way of showing care is to invest in them: in their education, health, and housing.

Access to assets provides a source of opportunities and capabilities. In this vein, Smith (2018) argues for asset-based assistance for high-risk children. Having identified children who are at high risk of future poverty (wards of the state), we would provide them with a reasonably generous cash endowment at the age of 18, so that they have the foundation for a positive start to their adult lives. The purposes for which this asset can be used for – such as education and skilling – would be strictly prescribed.

---

[145] Coote and Percy (2020).

What would I prioritise and why?

A give and care system (to paraphrase Banajee and Duflo's (2019) Cash and Care proposal) needs to be based on a strong partnership between central government, local and regional government, and communities. While cash will almost certainly be provided by the central government, most of the care will be delivered by the communities. However, equity and fairness are not a one-sided game. Every giving needs to be strongly conditional on need and effort on the part of the recipient.

This is where the localism discussion of chapter 6 and the governance proposals presented in chapter 5 are also critically important. A lot of investment in building capability in communities through major local and regional government involvement is needed. Provision of central government funding should be accompanied by a strict requirement of accountabilities for the delivery of targeted outcomes.

Complementary clean environment strategies would be implemented through a combination of taxes, regulations and subsidies (including research and development subsidies) to encourage the switch of both production and consumption towards cleaner technologies and products. Concurrently, through R&D support and related measures, such policies would encourage investment in and thereby increased supply of human capital in the form of skilled labour and scientists who can work with clean machines. This package of policies is developed in Acemoglu *et al.* (2012) and summarised in Karacaoglu *et al.* (2019).

Subsidies for education and skilling can also help reduce the inequality in the distribution of human capital. By reducing the inequality in the distribution of market income, we would also be decreasing the inequality in the ownership of physical and financial (bank) capital through the convergence of saving rates across these clusters of individuals.

An additional, critical, point was made very clearly by Sir Partha Dasgupta (2020). Population growth is one of the two main sources of stress on biodiversity, as well as the quality of the natural environment in general. The second one is the growth and composition of human consumption. In a democratic society, it is almost impossible to imagine natural population growth being controlled by state-imposed rules and regulations. The main alternative is to achieve this over time through education and social persuasion. Here too investment in education yields huge dividends.

Where is the reasoning and evidence to support these priorities?
The reasoning and evidence supporting various facets of this narrative are extremely well developed in Acemoglu and Robinson (2019), Banerjee and Duflo (2011, 2019), and Rajan (2019). Karacaoglu *et al.* (2019) provide an extensive survey of the associated literature. Appendix 2 of this book summarises some of the empirical literature supporting the narrative.

Figure 18 provides a summary of the outputs of some numerical simulations, using a simplified version of the stylised model discussed in Karacaoglu *et al.* (2019). The main purpose of that model is to demonstrate the interactions of environmental, social and economic factors in influencing wellbeing. All simulations are calculated over a twenty-year period. The purpose of these simulations is to explore and demonstrate the interactions of wealth, poverty reduction, social cohesion, output, technology and environmental quality, in affecting wellbeing.

Starting from the upper left-hand side of figure 18, the first diagram represents the interaction between average per capita real wealth and wealth-poverty. In these simulations, poverty is measured (or represented) by the percentage of people whose ownership of wealth, broadly defined, is below a certain thresh-

What would I prioritise and why?

Figure 18. Simulations demonstrating the workings of policy recommendations

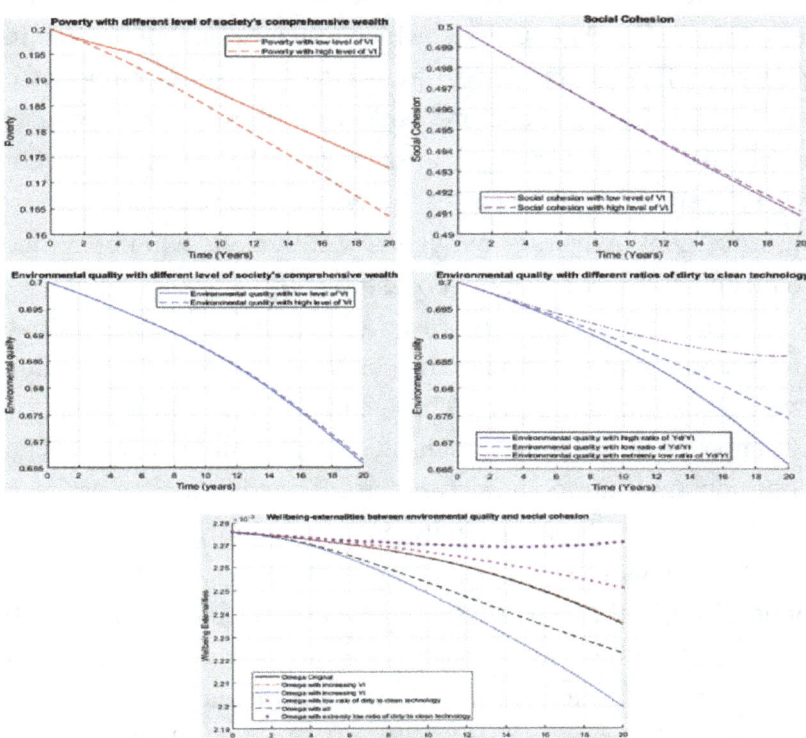

old. The source of our long-run data on wealth for New Zealand is Qasim *et al.* (2018).

The diagram highlights and captures the very slow impact of an overall average increase in wealth on reducing poverty, in line with the evidence provided in Qasim *et al.* (2018). The solid (dashed) poverty line is obtained with no impact of comprehensive wealth on reducing poverty. We note that poverty reduces from 20 percent to 19.2 percent over the twenty-year period due to policy-independent factors.

We then assume that average per capita wealth follows the

long-term improving trend shown in Qasim *et al.* (2018). We represent this trend numerically in this simulation as growth from $5,000 to $11,000 in 20 years, which assists a further decline in poverty to 16.4 percent – see the dashed line. So, in our model, a 6 percent p.a. growth of comprehensive wealth can reduce poverty by about 4 percentage points after 20 years (i.e. from 20 percent to 16.4 percent). This is consistent with our expectation that an improvement in average per capita wealth alone will not suffice to make a significant dent in poverty levels.

The second diagram represents the consequential positive impact on social cohesion of the positive influence of increasing average wealth on poverty. These calibrations are informed by Green *et al.* (2011) and Larsen (2014), who confirm that social cohesion (measured by survey-based proxies for generalised trust) is very sticky, especially when we control for the main influences (such as inequality of various types and corruption) on it. Thus, in the diagram, social cohesion declines by only 0.9 percentage points over twenty years, with the consequential improvement arising from the positive influence of increasing wealth on poverty being very marginal as well (dashed line).

The third diagram (the first diagram in the second row) depicts the consequential impact of an increase in comprehensive wealth on environmental quality. The rate of environmental improvement due to self-cleaning is modest. We note that, in this calibration, both the natural improvement in environmental quality (with no production – the solid line), and the consequential positive impact on environmental quality (through reduction in poverty) of an increase in average wealth (the dashed line), are small. The parameter estimates are informed by the projections provided in Conti *et al.* (2016) and related USA Energy Information Agency reports.

What would I prioritise and why?

We observe that the estimates characterise an economy with little environmental self-cleaning capacity and whose environmental quality is positively, albeit only mildly, related to poverty reduction.

In the fourth diagram, we do allow for the impact of production on environmental quality, that is we turn on the output impact. We assume that per capita output (or real income) grows from $32,000 to $100,000 over the twenty-year period. We proceed to study the impact, over a twenty-year period, of production with dirty and relatively clean technologies represented by the share of output produced by each type of technology. Overall, we observe that environmental degradation can be reversed only if supported by strong policies, like one that would result in a sixteen-fold decrease in the use of dirty technology – see the dashed line turning upwards.

In the last diagram, we bring all these influences together and assume that these various influences on wellbeing are of a complementary nature. In this figure we see five lines, each corresponding to a policy scenario that results in a different time profile of comprehensive wealth, output and technology improvement.

The fundamental point to note is that the largest positive impact on the externality multiplier on wellbeing results from a change in the composition of output. In other words, it happens as a result of the switch to cleaner technology in production and consumption.

It is also worth highlighting the positive impacts of a reduction in poverty, or increase in opportunity. Poverty reduction positively influences wellbeing through several, mutually-reinforcing, channels. It is good for the environment because poor people do not have the choices to consume environmental-friendly products. It is also good for social cohesion because poverty is a source of all kinds of social tensions. Through these impacts, it then creates a series of second-round positive influences on wellbeing, including social and environmental resilience.

Poverty-reducing or capability- and opportunity-enhancing measures provide examples of policy interventions that have multiple benefits. When dealing with multidimensional and mutually dependent environmental, social, and economic systems, these are the ideal types of interventions.

At an operational or management level, the distinctive features of a wellbeing approach to public management is well-summarised in the following table from Wallace (2019). The last column provides a useful summary of the main points in this book.

Table 3. Distinctive management features of a wellbeing approach

	Public administration	New public management	An emerging wellbeing approach
Aim	Welfare	Welfare	Wellbeing
Measurement	Input focus	Output focus	Outcomes focus
Structure	Silo based	Silo based	Horizontal integration (whole-of-government)
Management	Command and control	Command and control	Vertical integration (localism)
Service approach	Professional	Managerial	Participation
Interventions	Universal care services and welfare for those in need	Universal care services and welfare for those in need	Universal care services and support for those at risk (prevention)

9. Living well – circular wellbeing

Let us conclude by going back to the three questions posed in the preface:

- How are we to live?
- By what standards should we judge ourselves?
- For what virtues should we strive?

Throughout this book, these questions were addressed through the lens of public policy. But what about individual behaviour? Public policy cannot achieve its objectives unless human behaviour is aligned with these objectives. For example, if each of us lives a life that damages the natural environment, we cannot maintain or enhance *environmental quality*. If we each refuse to live in harmony with those from other backgrounds and cultures, we cannot achieve *social cohesion* in aggregate, and so on.

So what kind of individual behaviour and actions would be fully aligned with expanding the aggregate, collective wellbeing garden?

- Look after yourself, investing in yourself, in your own health, education and so on.
- Be fair in dealing with others.
- Minimise your activities that harm the natural environment.

| **Love you** – *Public policy for intergenerational wellbeing*

- 💙 Work hard.
- 💙 Build networks and social connections.
- 💙 Do not hurt others.
- 💙 Enjoy your freedom and passionately protect the freedoms of everyone else.

I have good news. *The science of wellbeing* suggests that, if we do live our lives in alignment with these principles, we will also achieve individual wellbeing – through enhanced resilience.[146]

We have thus discovered the recipe for *circular wellbeing*. Pursue a life that is fully aligned with expanding the social wellbeing garden, and you will have achieved personal wellbeing. Everybody, including unborn generations, wins.

Go well!!!

---

[146] Santos (2020).

10. Epilogue
Covid-19 – a wellbeing-focused policy response

This book was substantially completed before the Covid-19 pandemic rolled across the world. Although most unfortunate, Covid-19 provides a perfect platform and a great opportunity for implementing a public policy that is genuinely focused on enhancing intergenerational wellbeing.

The context

Covid-19 does not change the environmental, social and economic realities, and associated recent trends, faced in any country, New Zealand included. Some of these are highlighted in table 1 in this book. In fact, apart from providing a temporary relief from adverse environmental pressures, as well as a most welcome boost to social capital (the network of relationships across communities that support and strengthen societies)[147] Covid-19 has magnified all the other trends highlighted in the table. The broader costs of Covid-19 will be borne disproportionately by the young, the less skilled, the materially poor, and our Māori and Pasifika populations.

The threat

Table 1 represents the New Zealand image of global environmental, social and economic pandemics, as highlighted recently by

---

[147] Haldane (2020).

Angel Gurria (2019), though he did not use the word pandemic in that context. All this has been happening right under our nose for quite some time. For decades, scholars have been highlighting these emerging environmental and social catastrophes, and the response, if any, has been excruciatingly slow and disjointed.

Now we are faced with a health pandemic in the form of Covid-19. This too should not come as a total surprise. Scholars and practitioners had imagined and warned about the possibility of such a pandemic.[148] That too was not acted upon.

There are concerns that this health pandemic may provide a platform for, and morph into, an economic and social pandemic in the form of sustained unemployment.[149] This would be devastating, especially for young adults.

Frozen like a possum staring into the lights of a car speeding towards it, we had been staring into a perfect storm for quite some time.[150] We froze in front of the headlights primarily because we had divergent and conflicting interests.

Yet when the Covid-19 pandemic did eventuate, the response – certainly in New Zealand as well as some other countries – was prompt and decisive.

What is going on here? Why do we respond so promptly and aggressively when lives and livelihoods are immediately at risk, yet drag our feet when there are potential existential threats facing our society and the human species?[151]

It is partly about vested interests, power, politics, and voice – especially the lack of voice for the poor and for future generations. It is also about the different natural human reactions to the certainty of the immediate threat to identified lives versus

---
[148] Hoffower (2020), Rodrik (2020), Sanger *et al*. (2020).
[149] Tcherneva (2020).
[150] Roubini (2020).
[151] Stephenson (2020).

the uncertainty of future threats to statistical lives.[152] But it is primarily about the convergence of interests.

The opportunity
Covid-19 has created a once-in-a-generation opportunity to respond to all the existing and emerging threats highlighted above simultaneously, and in an integrated and coordinated way, serving all interests. It has done that precisely because the threat from this virus provided a catalyst for the convergence of a whole range of hitherto divergent interests.

Take Queenstown as a small example. For many years, a large part of the community had been agonising about the negative impacts of the excessive growth in tourism on the natural environment, as well as the social fabric of Queenstown. The weight of power rested with those interest groups (mainly business interests) that favoured the status quo. They continued to advocate for, and invest in economic infrastructures to accommodate, even larger tourist numbers.

Now that international tourism has dried up, and the status quo is no longer that lucrative, those same interests are gradually but surely joining the wider community in starting to imagine a world without large tourist numbers. Suddenly, people are imagining a Queenstown that may distinguish itself as an environmental haven to which intellectual capital (and their families) is attracted from around the world. It could be a place where brilliant ideas are incubated and then commercialised globally. It could possibly accommodate a world-class university of some sort. And so on.

This is very powerful stuff. It really does present a unique opportunity, not only for Queenstown but for New Zealand at

---
[152] Chaudhuri (2020).

large, and only because Covid-19 served as a catalyst for the convergence of disparate and conflicting interests.

The pertinent question now is, how do we convert this opportunity into productive action which then generates wellbeing-enhancing outcomes?

Framing of public policy objectives

Conversations around the potential consequences of Covid-19 around the world, as well as the evolution of various responses to it, have centred around lives and livelihoods, impacts on the natural environment, economic and fiscal implications, intergenerational considerations, democratic rights and personal liberties, as well as psycho-social (family, community, and wider) consequences.

Figure 4 captures all the key dimensions of these conversations around its perimeter. It conceptualises the primary purpose of a wellbeing-focused public policy as the enlargement of the wellbeing garden in which social life takes place, now and into the future.

All the 'pandemics' referred to earlier (including environmental and social ones) are creating pressures towards shrinking the wellbeing garden. Environmental quality, potential economic growth (that is, the material sources of wellbeing), social cohesion, personal freedoms and political voice and equity are now, or will soon be, under stress. The ecosystems that sit in the middle of the figure 4 are the areas where public policy should be investing, first to protect the garden from shrinking and second to expand it. Through such investments, we would be enhancing systemic resilience – both our capacity to absorb shocks, as well as our capabilities to recover following shocks.

Covid-19 – a wellbeing-focussed policy response

What should we do?
Worldwide efforts, including those in New Zealand, to contain and then eradicate the current health pandemic are underway. Like others, we are putting in place a range of immediate measures to protect jobs, incomes and cashflows as well as social welfare benefits.

In his Covid-19 press briefing on 24 April 2020, Minister of Finance Grant Robertson referred to three phases of the economic response to the pandemic: first, fighting the virus and cushioning the blow; second, positioning for recovery and kick-starting the economy; and third, resetting and rebuilding our economy.

This discussion is about phase three and our focus is broader than the economy. It is about 'laying the foundations for a better future', as the Governor-General expressed it in her speech from the throne on 26 November 2020. As a complement, and in addition to the first two phases of the response which are already well underway, here we have a unique opportunity to rethink and reshape our *long-term* investment strategy as a country.

This requires a highly integrated and inclusive approach. Integrated in the sense that infrastructure needs to include environmental, social and economic infrastructure. Inclusive, because we need a process by which all stakeholders, representing various layers of government, the private sector, NGOs, scientists, age groups and ethnicities are involved, from the imagining phase to full implementation and evaluation.

The long-term policy question is this: which of the ecosystems that sit in the middle of the wellbeing garden in figure 4 do we invest in, and in what priority (taking into account their complementarities), so that: first, we prevent the shrinkage; and second we prepare the ground for the actual expansion of the garden?

The strategic focus of our medium- to long-term response should be investing for sustainable employment creation in activities and industries – existing and to be collectively imagined – that are environment-friendly (Gurria 2020). This needs to be complemented by investments in human capital, that are targeted to upskilling the workforce so that they can be productively employed using the new technologies that these long-term investments will introduce into our environment-friendly production processes.

My proposed strategic focus on preventing unemployment and creating sustained, environment-friendly, employment at this very juncture has several foundations. First, unemployment (employment) has a major negative (positive) effect on wellbeing (Layard 2011). Second, Covid-19 has led to a convergence of diverse interests towards imagining futures with positive environmental, social and economic attributes. Third, in the absence of effective and acceptable short- and medium-term measures to control population growth, this is the best way of addressing our material needs without destroying the natural environment.[153]

Under this strategy, we would hit all the wellbeing buttons simultaneously: potential economic growth, equity, social cohesion, environmental quality, freedoms and political voice – all significant contributors to sustainable wellbeing. Provided, of course, that these long-term investments are directed towards switching our production processes towards using environmentally friendly technologies, and our consumption choices towards goods and services that are produced by these technologies.

The choice and prioritisation of specific investments to achieve these broad objectives cannot be done by central government. The role of central government is to create structures

---

[153] Dasgupta (2020).

and institutions that can harness and aggregate the collective wisdom of all stakeholders towards the choice and prioritisation of these investments.

How should we proceed?
Contrary to some emerging claims that current circumstances require reimagining the roles of the state and of markets[154], all that is required is creating an environment in which these institutions play their distinctive roles for the benefit of society – current and future.[155] As Chris Trotter (2020) puts it, 'the present crisis will cause the state to be recognised for what, historically, it has always been: the institutional expression of human interdependence: the place where everybody comes together, and nobody gets left behind'.

There is absolutely nothing wrong with the private sector, using institutions such as well-functioning markets as their instruments, making lots of profit. In fact it is essential that they do so – provided that these profits flow from activities which benefit society at large, current and future. One of the distinctive roles of government is to create the ecosystems for this to happen; again, see figure 4.

The governance and management steps that need to be followed[156] have been outlined and explained in chapter 5. So have appropriate funding mechanisms. No adjustments are required.

In terms of the step relating to a dedicated investment manager associated with each long-term outcome (in this case systemic investments that generate sustained employment growth while enhancing environmental quality), the New Zealand Infrastruc-

---

[154] E.G. Reddy (2020).
[155] Mazzucato (2013), Rajan (2019).
[156] Boston (2017 a, b), Boston (2019), Boston *et al.* (2019), Warren (2019).

ture Commission is ideally set up to play that role. The critical change that is required in the thinking of the Commission is to include in the definition of infrastructure, environmental, social, and economic infrastructure that serves intergenerational wellbeing, not just economic infrastructure.

Equally important is the process followed in prioritising and then deciding how we implement these investments. As already stated, they need to involve, in a spirit of genuine partnership, central and local governments, the scientific community, the private and public business sectors, NGOs, and representatives of various disciplines, ethnicities, and genders. Harnessing the collective imagination and wisdom of all these stakeholders, in prioritising the long-term investments as well as agreeing on a division of labour between them, is a critical role for the Commission to play.

In other words, the specific sets or combinations of investments that will achieve these outcomes, and the distinctive role of public policy (including public investments) in creating the required ecosystems to support these investments, will be determined by this cooperative process.

Not to be forgotten is funding arrangements. As I explained in chapter 5, referring to the mutual investment model adopted in Wales as an example, co-investment models reflecting private–public partnerships are common overseas.

New Zealand businesses are raring to go, to engage with government agencies, scientists and communities at large, to explore tomorrow's logic and opportunities.[157] Let us not miss this tremendous opportunity, generated by a global disaster, to imagine and build a better future.

---

[157] Drury (2020), Federated Farmers New Zealand (2020), Henley (2020), Tourism Industry Aotearoa (2020).

'In his discussion of managing turbulence, the father of modern-day management, Peter Drucker, noted the greatest danger in times of turbulence is not the turbulence; it is to act with yesterday's logic. ... Tackling "wicked problems" – complex and unsolvable social problems at the nexus of society and policy with no optimal solutions and unclear criteria – that have been exacerbated or exposed by Covid-19 requires stronger collective action, a higher degree of social agency and, above all, a shared sense of humanity.'[158]

---

[158] Rašković (2020).

Appendix 1
Evidence – institutions and wellbeing

Here we present some empirical evidence to highlight the critical role of institutions in the pursuit of intergenerational wellbeing.

Empirical evidence

For a review of the literature, including empirical evidence, on the interface between culture, institutions, and economic outcomes, see Alesina and Giuliano (2015) and Gorodnichenko and Roland (2011).

One of the main findings of this strand of literature is that 'individualistic cultures that place value on personal freedom, self-reliance, creative expression, affective autonomy, and reward individuals for their accomplishments with higher social status, tend to experience faster rates of innovation and economic growth compared to more collectivist societies'.[159]

For an early contribution regarding the positive impact of wellbeing for the development of good institutions, see Lipset (1959). Bennett *et al.* (2016) provides a useful and recent survey of related literature. Faria *et al.* (2016) provide further empirical evidence supporting the potential virtuous cycle between institutions and sources of wider wellbeing.

On the endogeneity of institutions in the long run, also see Rodrik (2004) and Acemoglu *et al.* (2005). This does not mean that

---

[159] Bennett *et al.* (2016), p9.

we are faced with a circularity that leads no room for deliberate policy. On this point, see the argument and evidence provided, among others, by Rodrik (2004), Acemoglu *et al.* (2014), Gründler and Krieger (2016), Sen (2009), and Sen (2017). Aidt (2009, 2011) provide examples of evidence on the negative effects of bad institutions on economic and social outcomes.

More to the point, given our specific focus on wider wellbeing, rather than exclusively on economic growth or material prosperity, is the relatively recent and emerging literature on the interface between formal and informal institutions, and wellbeing.

Recent studies have started examining the relationship between formal and cultural institutions, and a variety of other objective and subjective social outcomes such as trust, tolerance, crime, poverty, or subjective wellbeing. Berggren and Nilsson (2016), for example, find suggestive evidence that the institutions of economic freedom increase tolerance, measured by the willingness to, for example, let atheists and homosexuals speak, keep books in libraries, and be a college level teacher. These authors suggest that this relationship may work through reducing feelings of tension and conflict. In this sense, institutions may play a vital role in creating a non-discriminatory and inclusive environment that fulfils the basic psychological need for relatedness.

An important insight from this literature, for instance, is that institutions may have a positive impact on psychological wellbeing beyond their direct impact on a variety of socioeconomic outcomes, a concept known as procedural utility.[160] The idea here is that people care not merely about outcomes, but also about the processes that lead to these outcomes. Individuals, for instance, may experience a higher level of subjective wellbeing if they believe that they are treated in a way they consider just or

---

[160] See Frey *et al.* (2004).

Evidence – institutions and wellbeing

fair regardless of the material outcomes. For instance, the right to participate in the political process, measured by the extent of direct democratic rights across regions, is strongly correlated with subjective wellbeing.[161]

Nikolaev and Bennett (2016) show that people who live in countries with institutions consistent with the principles of economic freedom experience a greater perception of freedom of choice and control over their life. They furthermore find suggestive evidence that a potential mechanism that explains this relationship is the perception of procedural fairness and social mobility. An emerging literature on the relationship between formal institutions and subjective wellbeing also finds a positive correlation between the institutions of economic freedom and subjective wellbeing, most often proxied by survey measures of life satisfaction.[162]

---

[161] See Frey and Stutzer (2002).
[162] See Kešeljević and Spruk (2016). This general discussion is sourced from Bennett *et al.* (2016), pp11–12.

Appendix 2
Evidence – broader impacts of opportunity on wellbeing

Here we present empirical evidence on how policies that emphasise anti-poverty (or increasing capabilities and opportunities) influence wellbeing at large through various channels.

The role of a citizen-centred public policy is to support people and communities in their efforts to improve their lives by enhancing their opportunities and capabilities – their substantive freedoms – to pursue the lives they have reason to value, while respecting and celebrating the diversity of valued lives. In a country where different communities, cities and regions are prospering, potentially in very different ways, people have far wider opportunities to live the kinds of lives they want to live, without leaving the country.

In the context of a very useful distinction between people's revealed preferences across personal-choice scenarios and policy-choice scenarios, Benjamin *et al.* (2014) provide survey-based empirical evidence on the relatively high rating given by respondents to policy-choice scenarios that, broadly speaking, provide opportunities and capabilities for individuals to live the kinds of lives they have reason to value.

A useful summary of the measures used to capture multidimensional poverty can be found in Toledo *et al.* (2016). A set of policy recommendations to reduce multidimensional poverty are provided by Atkinson (2015) and Boston and Chapple (2014).

Poverty-reducing and opportunity – increasing measures provide examples of policy interventions that have multiple benefits. These are the ideal types of interventions when we are dealing with multidimensional and mutually dependent environmental, social and economic systems.

Breunig and Majeed (2016) provide empirical evidence in support of their policy advice to reduce inequality by attacking poverty rather than by redistributing income, on the basis that this has a wider positive impact on wellbeing through its positive impact on potential economic growth, the quality of institutions, and social cohesion.

Poverty reduction positively influences wellbeing through several, mutually-reinforcing, channels. It is good for the environment because poor people do not have the choices to consume environmental-friendly products. It is also good for social cohesion because poverty is a source of all kinds of social tensions. Through these impacts, it then creates a series of second-round positive influences on wellbeing, including social and environmental resilience.

A very useful survey of the literature on poverty, inequality, economic growth, and social cohesion is provided by Breunig and Majeed (2016). The same paper also provides empirical evidence on the interface between inequality, poverty and economic growth, and concludes that when poverty is low, the relationship between inequality and economic growth is statistically insignificant. As the level of poverty increases, so does the negative effect of inequality on economic growth. It also emphasises, however, that both poverty and inequality can and do negatively impact wellbeing through other channels as well, including a decrease in social cohesion and a deterioration in the quality of institutions.

Welsch and Biermann (2017) provide empirical evidence in

| Evidence – broader impacts of opportunity on wellbeing

support of the hypothesis that poverty, like unemployment, is not only a 'private bad', but also a 'public bad'. Not only personally being poor (unemployed), but also the aggregate level of poverty (unemployment) negatively affects subjective wellbeing, especially of those who are not poor themselves. In both cases, 'people may be unhappy about poverty (unemployment) even if they are not poor (unemployed) themselves. They may feel bad about the unfortunate fate of the poor (unemployed) and they may worry about the possibility of becoming poor (unemployed) themselves in the future. They may also feel repercussions on the economy and on society at large. They may dislike the increase in taxes likely to happen in the future. They may fear that crime and social tensions increase, and they may even see the threat of violent protests and uprisings.'[163] The latter reference refers to concerns about the potential negative link between poverty and social cohesion.

Parallel references to unemployment are from Frey and Stutzer (2002). Corresponding evidence regarding unemployment is presented in Di Tella, *et al.* (2001).

Acemoglu and Robinson (2000) and Yamamura (2016) provide theoretical arguments and empirical evidence in support of the proposition that high-income earners' support and stated preference for income redistribution relates to their concern about the potential conflict between the rich and the poor, that is the erosion of social cohesion.

In addition, as Welsch and Biermann (2017) point out: 'From a policy point of view, the finding that poverty is a public bad and/or creates negative externalities suggests that poverty implies market failure. This, in turn, suggests that poverty alleviation is a matter not only of equity, but of efficiency.'[164]

---

[163] Ibid., p2.
[164] p9.

Angelopoulos *et al.* (2017) provide a very useful survey of the literature, particularly in the context of the UK, on whether job-related training targeted at low-skilled workers helps increase income and reduce the inequality of income between skilled and unskilled workers, as well as conducting their own independent empirical investigation. They find that while subsidising job-related training for unskilled workers does lead to an increase in their income, it has only a modest impact on reducing income inequality between unskilled and skilled labour because it has a positive spillover effect on skilled labour as well, thus increasing overall income by increasing the earnings of both unskilled and skilled labour.

Sachs (2015) notes that 'societies with high social capital outperform those with low social capital in terms of subjective wellbeing (SWB) and economic development'.[165] In this context, empirical evidence, which also has implications for public policy, is more nuanced.

Pervaiz and Chaudhary (2015) argue and provide both a theoretical rationale and empirical evidence to support their argument, that different dimensions of social cohesion have different impacts on economic and social outcomes. Strong within-group social cohesion, associated with bonding capital, to the extent that it is divisive, discriminatory, and exclusive can have negative effects on trust, democratic institutions, political and social stability, and transaction costs, thus having negative implications for social and economic outcomes. On the other hand, strong across-group social cohesion, associated with bridging capital, by underpinning and supporting the formation of strong institutions, generalised trust, collaboration, lower transaction costs, and innovation, can have a very positive impact on social and economic outcomes.

When it comes to subjective wellbeing (or life satisfaction, or

---

[165] p152.

Evidence – broader impacts of opportunity on wellbeing

happiness), on the other hand, Growiec *et al.* (2017) cite a range of studies 'confirming the importance of maintaining frequent social interactions, both with similar and dissimilar others, for individuals' life satisfaction and happiness'.[166]

Another study that finds strong, positive, and lasting correlations between diversity and economic development is Rodríguez-Pose and von Berlepsch (2019). Examining the USA and comparing the experiences of states and counties across the country, they:

> 'identify the presence of a strong and very long-lasting impact of diversity on county-level economic development. Counties that attracted migrants from very diverse national and international origins over a century ago are significantly richer today than those that were marked by a more homogeneous population at the time. [...] Yet the benefits of diversity came with a strong caveat: the gains of having a large number of groups from different origins within a territory (fractionalization) only materialise if the diverse groups are able to communicate with one another (low polarisation). Deep cut lines separating the groups (high polarisation) emerge as an important barrier for economic development.
>
> 'Hence, diversity becomes a double-edged sword: it works only if the different groups can interact, that is, if the "melting pot" really happens. Where it is not possible to build a dialogue between the different groups, where bridging does not occur, groups and communities remain in their own physical or mental ghettoes, undermining any economic benefits from a diverse environment.'[167]

---

[166] p11.
[167] pp885–886.

There is also a growing empirical literature on the relationship between the income and socioeconomic characteristics of individual households and the carbon content of their consumption. According to the literature survey conducted by Berthe and Elie (2015), there does not appear to be a systematic relationship between inequality of income and pollution. Sager (2017) attributes this partly to the limitations of drawing such inferences from cross-country studies.

When he then attempts to quantify the equity-pollution dilemma using micro-data on household consumption within a single country (the USA), controlling for the scale (income and level of consumption), composition (preferences), and technology effects on consumption baskets, he finds 'Environmental Engel Curves (EECs) for CO_2 to be upward-sloping, concave, and shifting downwards overtime' (ibid., p1). And then, 'Given the higher pollution intensity of consumption per expenditure by poorer households, progressive redistribution [of income] may result in higher aggregate pollution from consumption.'[168]

Example of an anti-poverty programme in action: Familias en Acción Urbano

This example is sourced from Galama *et al.* (2017). They start by acknowledging with references to the literature that:

> '...it is unclear whether anti-poverty programs can have lasting impacts on economic wellbeing, subjective wellbeing and self sufficiency, while mitigating the costs to taxpayers. Critics argue, for example, that anti-poverty programs are costly redistribution programs that promote government dependency through reduced work incentives [...]

---

[168] Ibid., p34.

'Alternatively, these programs may expand participants' choice sets (e.g. through improved nutrition) enabling them to take advantage of labour-market opportunities, and by increasing self-sufficiency, reduce the burden on taxpayers.'[169]

They then go on to report:

'We empirically address this question in the context of Familias en Acción Urbano (FAU), a conditional cash transfer program implemented at scale in the country of Colombia.

'FAU targets socioeconomically disadvantaged households in Colombia's fourteen largest cities, which concentrate over 80% of the country's population. At full scale, Familias en Acción (rural plus urban expansion) benefits over two million households nationwide.

'For eligible households, FAU provides cash transfers to families with children under the age of 18 conditional on medical visits for younger children and school enrolment and continued attendance for secondary school students. We take advantage of the fact that a means-test score determines FAU eligibility. As we demonstrate with the aid of administrative baseline data, the means-test score provides exogenous variation in program participation near the program eligibility cut off.

'We then reproduce the means-test score assignment rule in a nationally representative Colombian living standards household survey collected three years into the program. The survey measures multiple dimensions of evaluative wellbeing as well as more objective measures that include income, consumption, health and education, and that lacks the incentives

---
[169] Ibid., p2.

for strategic reporting because it was not designed to explicitly target program beneficiaries or track program-related outcomes.'[170]

'Three years into the program, beneficiary households at the margin of eligibility report greater income, consumption and formal employment participation for both household head and partner. Impacts on household income at the margin are a factor of ten times greater than would be expected solely on the basis of the cash transfers, likely because of gains in formal employment.

'This finding casts doubt on the notion that anti-poverty programs always generate work disincentives and is consistent with recent evidence from other cash transfer programs. [...] Increases in consumption that result from program participation map almost one to one to increases in income, and there is a substantial increase on food expenditures among beneficiary households at the margin, which may have influenced the quantity and quality of nutritional intakes.

'Through enhanced choice sets, anti-poverty programs like Colombia's conditional cash transfer program may open new avenues for increased market opportunities among beneficiary households.'[171]

'To summarise, our main contribution to this nascent literature is threefold. We document how a conditional cash transfer anti-poverty program can simultaneously improve material and subjective conditions for participants and increase their self sufficiency.

---

[170] Ibid., p2.
[171] Ibid., p3.

Evidence – broader impacts of opportunity on wellbeing

'By simultaneously measuring objective and subjective measures of wellbeing our results may shed light on potential pathways by which anti-poverty programs can improve wellbeing among households with unmet needs. Second, our findings suggest that those goals can sometimes be achieved at a reduced cost to taxpayers, to the extent that anti-poverty programs help enhance participants' market opportunities.'[172]

---

[172] Ibid., p5.

References

Acemoglu, Daron (2019). 'Why a Universal Basic Income is a bad idea', *Project Syndicate*; 7 June 2019.

Acemoglu, Daron; Johnson, Simon; Robinson, James A. (2005). 'Institutions as a Fundamental Cause of Long-run Growth' in: P. Aghion and S. N. Durlauf, eds. *Handbook of Economic Growth*, 1, 385–472. Elsevier.

Acemoglu, Daron; Aghion, Philippe; Bursztyn, Leonardo; and Hemous, David (2012). 'The Environment and Directed Technical Change.' *The American Economic Review*. Vol 102, pp131–166.

Acemoglu, Daron and Robinson, James A. (2000). 'Why did the West Extend the Franchise? Democracy, Inequality, and Growth in Historical Perspective.' *The Quarterly Journal of Economics*, 115, 1167–1199.

Acemoglu, Daron and Robinson, James A. (2013). *Why Nations Fail: The Origins of Power, Prosperity, and Poverty*. New York: Crown Business.

Adler, Matthew D and Fleurbaey, Marc (2016), eds. *The Oxford Handbook of Wellbeing and Public Policy*. Oxford: Oxford University Press.

Aidt, Toke S. (2009). 'Corruption, Institutions, and Economic Development.' *Oxford Review of Economic Policy*, 25, 271–291.

Agar, Nicholas (2020). "Aotearoa needs a truly inclusive Ministry for the Future," *Newsroom*. 5 November.

Aidt, Toke S. (2011). 'Corruption and Sustainable Development.' in S. Rose-Ackerman and T. Søreide, eds. *International Handbook on the Economics of Corruption*, Volume 2, pp3–51. Cheltenham UK: Edward Elgar.

Alesina, Alberto and Giuliano, Paola (2015). 'Culture and Institutions'. *Journal of Economic Literature*, 53, 898–944.

Alexander, Michael (2019). 'Cross-party group of MPs formed to advocate for mental health', *Newshub*, 28 August.

Alkire, Sabina (2002). *Valuing Freedoms: Sen's Capability Approach and Poverty Reduction*. New York: Oxford University Press. doi:10.1093/0199245797.003.0001

Alkire, Sabina (2005). 'Why the Capability Approach?'. *Journal of Human Development*, 6(1), 115-135. doi:10.1080/146498805200034275

Angelopoulos, Konstantinos; Benecchi, Andrea; Malley, Jim (2017). 'Can Subsidising Job-related Training Reduce Inequality?'. *CESifo Working Paper* No. 6605.

Arthur, W. Brian (2014). *Complexity and the Economy*. Oxford: Oxford University Press.

Arvanitidis, Paschalis (2004). 'The Diverse Traditions of Institutional Economics: Conceptual and Methodological Underpinnings'. University of Thessaly, Greece, *Discussion Paper Series*, 10, 317–50.

Atkinson, Anthony B. (2015). *Inequality*. Cambridge: Harvard University Press.

Bache, Ian and Reardon, Louise (2016). *The Politics and Policy of Wellbeing – Understanding the Rise and Significance of a New Agenda*. Edward Elgar Publishing.

Banerjee, Abhijit V. and Duflo, Esther (2011). *Poor Economics*. London: Penguin Books.

Banerjee, Abhijit V. and Duflo, Esther (2019). *Good Economics for Hard Times*. London: Penguin Books.

Beinhocker, Eric (2016). 'How the Profound Changes in Economics Make Left versus Right Debates Irrelevant'. *Evonomics*. 26 May.

Belgrave, Michael (2004). 'Needs and the State: Evolving Social Policy in New Zealand History'. In B. Dalley and M. Tennant (eds.), *Past Judgement: Social policy in New Zealand History* (pp23–38). Dunedin: University of Otago Press.

Benjamin, Daniel J.; Heffetz, Ori; Kimball, Miles S.; Szembrot, Nichole (2014). 'Beyond Happiness and Satisfaction: Toward Well-being Indices Based on Stated Preference.' *The American Economic Review*, 104, 2698–2735.

Benjamin, Walter (1996). *Walter Benjamin, Selected Writings Volume 1, 1913–1926* (Belknap Press of Harvard University Press, Cambridge, MA: 1996). Translated by Rodney Livingstone.

Bennett, Daniel L.; Nikolaev, Boris; and Aidt, Toke S. (2016). 'Institutions and Well-being'. *European Journal of Political Economy*, Vol 45 (supplement), pp 1–10.

References

Berggren, Niclas and Nilsson, Therese (2016). 'Tolerance in the United States: Does Economic Freedom Transform Racial, Religious, Political and Sexual Attitudes?' *European Journal of Political Economy*, 45, 50–70.

Berthe, Alexandre and Elie, Luc (2015). 'Mechanisms Explaining the Impact of Economic Inequality on Environmental Deterioration'. *Ecological Economics*, 116, 191–200.

Bertram, Geoff and Terry, Simon (2013). *Green Border Control: Issues at the Environment/Economy Border*. Prepared for Royal Forest and Bird Protection Society of New Zealand Inc. by Simon Terry Associates.

Boarini, Romina and d'Ercole, Marco Mira (2013). 'Going beyond GDP: An OECD Perspective'. *Fiscal Studies*, 34, 289–314.

Boarini, Romina; Kolev, Alexandra; McGregor, Allister (2014), 'Measuring well-being and progress in countries at different stages of development: Towards a more universal conceptual framework', *OECD Development Centre Working Papers*, No. 325, OECD Publishing, Paris.

Boston, Jonathan (2017 a). *Safeguarding the Future – Governing in an Uncertain World*. BWB Texts.

Boston, Jonathan (2017 b). *Governing for the Future – Designing Democratic Institutions for a Better Tomorrow*. Emerald.

Boston, Jonathan (2019). *Transforming the Welfare State – towards a new social contract*. BWB Texts.

Boston, Jonathan; Bagnall, David; and Barry, Anna (2019). *Foresight, Insight and Oversight: Enhancing Long-Term Governance through Better Parliamentary Practices*. Institute for Governance and Policy Studies.

Boston, Jonathan and Chapple, Simon (2014). *Child Poverty in New Zealand*. BWB Texts.

Breuer, Anita; Janetschek, Hannah; Malerba, Daniele (2019). 'Translating Sustainable Goal (SDG) Interdependencies into Policy Advice', *Sustainability*, 11, 2–20.

Breunig, Robert and Majeed, Omer (2016). 'Inequality or Poverty: Which is Bad for Growth?' *Centre for Applied Macroeconomic Analysis Working Paper* 43/2016, Canberra, Australian Capital Territory.

Broadberry, Stephen and Wallis, John (2017). 'Growing, Shrinking, and Long Run Economic Performance: Historical Perspectives on Economic Development'. *Technical Report*. National Bureau of Economic Research.

Brown, Marie A (2017). *Last Line of Defence*. Wellington: Environmental Defence Society.

Burns, Danny and Howard, Jo (2018). 'Leaving No-one Behind: Building Sustainable Inclusion [Online Lecture]. https://www.ids.ac.uk/events/leave-no-one-behind-building-sustainable-inclusion/

Burns, Danny and Worsley, Stuart (2015). *Navigating Complexity in International Development: Facilitating Sustainable Change at Scale*. Rugby: Practical Action Publishing. doi:10.3362/9781780448510

Cadogan, Bernard (2013). 'Welfare Policy: Governance History and Political Philosophy,' *New Zealand Treasury Working Papers*. July. Wellington.

Camfield, Laura (2006). 'Why and How of Understanding "Subjective" Wellbeing: Exploratory work by the WeD group in four developing countries'. (Working Paper 26). https://ueaeprints.uea.ac.uk/id/eprint/24946/

Campiglio, Emanuele (2016). 'Beyond Carbon Pricing: The Role of Banking and Monetary Policy in Financing the Transition to a Low-Carbon Economy'. *Ecological Economics*, 121, 220–230.

Carattini, Stefano and Roesti, Matthias (2020). 'Trust, Happiness, and Pro-Social Behavior', *cesifo Working Papers*. No. 8562, September.

Carlin, Wendy and Bowles, Samuel (2017). *CORE – Economics for a Changing World*. CORE eBook.

Cecil, Wes (several). *Forgotten Thinkers Series*. YouTube. wescecil.com/forgotten-thinkers

Chakravarty, Satya and Lugo, Maria Ana (2016). 'Multidimensional Indicators of Inequality and Poverty'. In: M. D. Adler and M. Fleurbaey, eds. *The Oxford Handbook of Well-being and Public Policy*. Oxford: Oxford University Press.

Chaudhuri, Ananish (2020). 'A Different Perspective on Covid-19'. *Newsroom*. 8 April.

Chertow, Marian R. (2008). 'The IPAT Equation and its Variants', *Journal of Industrial Ecology*. 8 February. https://doi.org/10.1162/10881980052541927

Clark, David A. (2005). 'Sen's Capability Approach and the Many Spaces of Human Wellbeing'. *Journal of Development Studies*, 41(8), 1339–1368. doi:10.1080/00220380500186853

Coleman, Andrew (2018). 'Public Submission to the Tax Working Group'. *Tax Working Group*.

References

Conti, John; Holtberg, Paul; Diefenderfer, Jim; LaRose, Angelina; Turnure, James T.; Westfall, Lynn (2016). *International Energy Outlook 2016 with Projections to 2040*. Technical Report. USDOE Energy Information Administration (EIA), Washington, DC (United States). Office of Energy Analysis.

Coote, Anna and Percy, Andrew (2020). *The Case for Universal Basic Services*. Polity.

Costanza, Robert; de Groot, Rudolf; Braat, Leon; Kubiszewski, Ida; Fioramonti, Lorenzo; Sutton, Paul C.; Farber, Steve; Grasso, Monica (2017). 'Twenty Years of Ecosystem Services: How far have we come and how far do we still need to go?'. *Ecosystem Services*, Vol 28, pp 1–16.

Coyle, Diane (2014). 'Measuring Economic Progress'. *VOX CEPR Policy Portal*, 17 February.

Coyle, Diane. (2015). *GDP: A Brief but Affectionate History*. Princeton: Princeton University Press.

Crampton, Eric and Acharya, Khyaati (2015). *In the Zone: Creating a Toolbox for Regional Prosperity*. Wellington: The New Zealand Initiative.

Crouch, Colin (2020). *Post-Democracy After the Crises*. Cambridge: Polity Press. [Wiley: Kindle Edition]

Dalley, Bronwyn and Tennant, Margaret (eds.) (2004). *Past Judgement: Social Policy in New Zealand History*. Dunedin: University of Otago Press.

Dalziel, Paul and Saunders, Caroline (2014). *Wellbeing Economics: Future Directions for New Zealand* (G. Walker Ed.). Wellington: Bridget Williams Books Limited.

Darwin, Charles (2003). *The Origin of Species*. 150th Anniversary Edition. Kindle.

Dasgupta, Partha (2020). 'The Economics of Biodiversity', *Reserve Bank of New Zealand Fellowship Lecture*. Victoria University of Wellington, 18 March.

De Long, J, Bradford (1998). 'Estimates of World GDP, One Million B.C. – Present', Department of Economics, U.C. Berkeley.

De Perthuis, Christian and Jouvet, Pierre-Andre (2015). *Green Capital: A New Perspective on Growth*. New York: Columbia University Press.

Dennett, Hartley (2018). 'Labor pledges new evaluator-general as program experts' friendly collaborator', *The Mandarin*. 13 November. https://www.themandarin.com.au/101279-labor-pledges-new-evaluator-general-as-program-experts-friendly-collaborator

Dietz, Thomas; Ostrom, Elinor; and Stern Paul C (2003). 'The Struggle to Govern the Commons', *Science* 302.

Di Tella, Rafael; MacCulloch, Robert. J.; Oswald, Andrew J. (2001). 'Preferences over Inflation and Unemployment: Evidence from Surveys of Happiness'. *The American Economic Review*, 91, 335–341.

Dorn, David; Fischer, Justina A. V.; Kirchgassner, Gebhard; and Sousa-Poza, Alfonso (2007). 'Is It Culture or Democracy? The Impact of Democracy and Culture on Happiness'. *Social Indicators Research*, 82(3), 505-526. doi:10.1007/s11205-006-9048-4.

Drury, Rod (2020). 'Covid-19 – What we do now will shape New Zealand's future', *Newsroom*. 13 April.

Erlingsson, Gissur O (2020). 'A Stranger Thing? Sweden – the Upside Down of Multilevel Trust', *IFN Working Paper*, No. 1356; September.

Evans, Lewis; Grimes, Arthur; Wilkinson, Bryce (1996). "Economic Reform in New Zealand 1984-95: Te Pursuit of Efficiency," *Journal of Economic Literature*. Vol. 34, issue 4, pp 1856-1902.

Evans, Lewis; Quigley, Neil; Guthrie, Graeme (2012). 'Contemporary Microeconomic Foundations for the Structure and Management of the Public Sector', *New Zealand Treasury Working Papers* (WP 12/01); July.

Evans, Lewis; Quigley, Neil (2013). 'Intergenerational Contracts and Time Consistency: Implications for Policy Settings and Governance in the Social Welfare System', *New Zealand Treasury Working Paper* (13/25). December.

Fals-Borda, Orlando and Rahman, Muhammad Anisur (eds.). (1991). *Action and Knowledge: Breaking the Monopoly with Participatory Action-Research*. London: Intermediate Technology Publications.

Faria, Hugo J.; Montesinos-Yufa, Hugo M; Morales, Daniel R; and Navarro, Carlos E. (2016). 'Unbundling the Roles of Human Capital and Institutions in Economic Development'. *European Journal of Political Economy*, 45, 108–128.

Federated Farmers New Zealand (2020). 'Smart Green Growth Requires Investment', *Media Release*. 8 April.

Fisher, Irving (1936). *Money*. Adelphi Company.

Fleurbaey, Marc and Blanchet, Didier (2013). *Beyond GDP: Measuring Welfare and Assessing Sustainability*. Oxford: Oxford University Press.

Freire, Paulo (1970). *Pedagogy of the Oppressed*. New York: Continuum.

References

Frey, Bruno S.; Benz, Matthias; and Stutzer, Alois (2004). 'Introducing Procedural Utility: Not Only What, but also How Matters'. *Journal of Institutional and Theoretical Economics JITE*, 160, 377–401.

Frey, Bruno S. and Stutzer, Alois (2002). 'What can Economists Learn from Happiness Research?' *Journal of Economic Literature*, 40, 402–435.

Frijters, Paul; Clark, Andrew E.; Krekel, Christian; Layard, Richard (2019). 'A Happy Choice: Wellbeing as the Goal of Government', *CEP Discussion Paper*, No 1658 (October).

Fujiwara, Daniel and Dolan, Paul (2016). 'Happiness Based Public Policy'. In: M. Adler and M. Fleurbaey (eds.) *The Oxford Handbook of Well-being and Public Policy*. Oxford: Oxford University Press; pp286–320.

Future Generations Commissioner, Wales (2020). https://futuregenerations.wales/about-us/future-generations-commissioner

Galama, Titus J.; Morgan, Robson; and Saavedra, Juan E. (2017). 'Wealthier, Happier and More Self-Sufficient: When Anti-Poverty Programs Improve Economic and Subjective Wellbeing at a Reduced Cost to Taxpayers'. *Technical Report*. National Bureau of Economic Research.

Gasper, Des (2009). 'Understanding the diversity of conceptions of well-being and quality of life'. *Journal of socio-economics*, 39(3), 351-360. doi:10.1016/j.socec.2009.11.006.

Gorodnichenko, Yuriy and Roland, Gerard (2011). 'Which dimensions of culture matter for long-run growth?' *The American Economic Review*, 101, 492–498.

Gough, Ian; McGregor, J. Allister; Camfield, Laura (2007). 'Theorising Wellbeing in International Development'. In I. Gough and J. A. McGregor (eds.), *Wellbeing in Developing Countries: from Theory to Research* (pp3–44). Cambridge: Cambridge University Press.

Government of the Netherlands (2016). *A Circular Economy in the Netherlands by 2050*. Government of the Netherlands.

Green, Andy; Janmaat, Germ; and Cheng, Helen (2011). 'Social Cohesion: Converging and Diverging Trends'. *National Institute Economic Review*, 215, R6–R22.

Greenaway-McGrevy, Ryan; Grimes, Arthur; Maloney, Tim; Bardsley, Anne; and Gluckman, Peter (2020). *New Zealand's economic future: Covid-19 as a catalyst for innovation*. Koi Tū: The Centre for Informed Futures, The University of Auckland. November.

Ryan Greenaway-McGrevy, Ryan; Grimes, Arthur; Maloney, Tim; Bardsley, Anne; and Gluckman, Peter (2020). *New Zealand's Economic Future: Covid-19 as a Catalyst for Innovation*. Koi Tū: The Centre for Informed Futures, The University of Auckland. November.

Griggs, David; Stafford-Smith, Mark; Gaffney, Owen; Rockström, Johan; Öhman, Marcus C.; Shyamsundar, Priya; Steffen, Will; Glaser, Gisbert; Kanie, Norichika; Noble, Ian (2013). 'Policy: Sustainable Development Goals for People and Planet'. *Nature*, 495, 305–307.

Growiec, Katarzyna; Growiec, Jakub; and Kamiński, Bogumil (2017). 'Mapping the Dimensions of Social Capital'. *SGH KAE Working Paper Series*, No. 2017/025.

Gründler, Klaus and Krieger, Tommy (2016). 'Democracy and Growth: Evidence from a Machine Learning Indicator'. *European Journal of Political Economy*, 45, 85–107.

Gurria, Angel (2019). 'Opening Remarks', *Putting Well-being Metrics into Policy Action*. OECD international workshop (2–4 October 2019).

Gurria, Angel (2020). 'An Inclusive, Green Recovery is Possible – The Time to Act is Now', *Statement by the OECD Secretary General*. 24 April. http://www.oecd.org/coronavirus/en/?utm_source=Adestra&utm_medium=email&utm_content=SG%20Statement&utm_campaign=What%27s%20New%20-%2024%20April%202020&utm_term=demo#statement

Haldane, Andrew G. (2015). 'Growing, Fast and Slow'. Speech at the University of East Anglia, Norwich, 17 February.

Haldane, Andrew G. (2018). 'Ideas and Institutions – A Growth Story'. *Bank of England Speech*. The Guild Society. University of Oxford.

Haldane, Andy (2020). 'Reweaving the social fabric after the crisis', *Financial Times*. 24 April.

Haldane, Andrew G. and May, Robert M. (2011). 'Systemic Risk in Banking Ecosystems'. *Nature*, 469, 351–5.

Hagens, Nate J. (2020). 'Economics for the Future: Beyond the Superorganism', *Ecological Economics*. Vol 169 (March), 106520. (https://doi.org/10.1016/j.ecolecon.2019.106520)

Hayek, Friedrich A. (2013). *The Constitution of Liberty*. Abingdon: Routledge.

References

Helliwell, John H. (2019). 'Measuring and Using Happiness to Support Public Policies', *NBER Working Paper Series*, December 2019.

Helliwell, John H.; Layard, Richard; Sachs, Jeffrey D.; De Neve, Jan-Emmanuel (2019). *World Happiness Report*. United Nations Sustainable Development Solutions Network.

Henley, Belinda (2020). 'Rocket man: Don't waste the crisis', *Newsroom*. 21 April.

Hey, Nancy (2019). 'Building the Evidence Base and Civil Service Capacity'. Presentation at the OECD international workshop on *Putting Well-being Metrics into Policy Action* (2-4 October 2019), Paris.

HM Treasury (2018). *The Green Book – Central Government Guidance on Appraisal and Evaluation*. UK: HM Treasury.

Hickey, Samuel and Mohan, Giles (eds.). (2004). *Participation, from Tyranny to Transformation? – Exploring New Approaches to Participation in Development*. New York: Palgrave Macmillan.

Hodgson, Geoffrey, M. (2006). 'What are Institutions?'. *Journal of Economic Issues*, Vol 40, pp 1–24.

Hoffower, Hillary (2020). 'Bill Gates has been warning of a global health threat for years. Here are 11 people who seemingly predicted the coronavirus pandemic.' *Business Insider Australia*. 21 March.

Hunt, Lynn (2007). *Inventing Human Rights: A History*. New York: W.W. Norton & Company.

Hunt, Tom and Peachey, Bevan (2020). 'Private sector investors can make major contribution to NZ infrastructure', *nzherald.co.nz*. 20 November.

Inspiring Communities (2020). *Shaping the Future – enabling community-led change*. Inspiring Communities

Investopedia (2019). 'Government & Policy The Nordic Model: Pros and Cons', https://www.investopedia.com/articles/investing/100714/nordic-model-pros-and-cons.asp – 25 Jun 2019

IRD and NZ Treasury (2018). *Distributional Analysis – Background Paper for Session 5 of the Tax Working Group*. Tax Working Group.

James, Colin (2020). '"Social Laboratory": Myth or Reality?'. In: Berman, Evan and Karacaoglu, Girol (eds). *Public Policy and Governance Frontiers in New Zealand*. Emerald Group.

Jara, H. Xavier and Schokkaert, Erik (2016). 'Putting Subjective Well-being to Use for Ex-ante Policy Evaluation', *Euromod Working Paper Series*, EM 9/16, December.

Karacaoglu, Girol; King, Anita; Krawczyk, Jacek B (2019). *Intergenerational Wellbeing and Public Policy – an integrated environmental, social, and economic framework*. Springer.

Kaufman, Walter (1961). *The Faith of a Heretic*. Princeton University Press.

Kay, John and King, Mervyn (2020). *Radical Uncertainty – Decision-Making Beyond the Numbers*. W.W. Norton & Company.

Kešeljević, Aleskandar and Spruk, Rok (2016). 'Institutional Origins of Subjective Well-being: Estimating the Effects of Economic Freedom on National Happiness'. *Journal of Happiness Studies*, 17, 659–712.

Keynes, John M (1935), *The General Theory of Employment, Interest and Money*, ch. 24, p383.

King, Mervyn (2016). *The End of Alchemy: Money, Banking, and the Future of the Global Economy*. New York: W.W. Norton & Company.

Krumdieck, Susan (2020). *Transition Engineering – building a sustainable future*. CRC Press.

Larsen, Christian Albrekt (2014). 'Social Cohesion: Definition, Measurement and Developments'. *WorkingPaper*, Institut for Statskundskab, Aalborg Universitet.

Layard, Richard (2011). *Happiness – Lessons from a New Science* (Second Edition). Penguin Books.

Layard, Richard and O'Donnell, Gus (2015). 'How to make policy when happiness is the goal'. In: *World Happiness Report*; edited by John F Helliwell, Richard Layard, and Jeffrey D Sachs; pp76–87; Sustainable Development Solutions Network, New York.

Lipset, Seymour Martin (1959). 'Some Social Requisites of Democracy: Economic Development and Political Legitimacy'. *The American Political Science Review*, 53, 69–105.

MacCulloch, Robert (2016). 'Can "happiness data" help evaluate economic policies?'. *Motu Working Paper* 16–02. Motu Economic and Public Policy Research. February.

Martin, Ian W. R. and Pindyck, Robert S. (2015). 'Averting catastrophes: The strange economics of Scylla and Charybdis'. *The American Economic Review*, 105, 2947–2985.

Maslow, Abraham (1943). 'A Theory of Human Motivation', *Psychological Review*, 50 (4): 370–96.

References

Mazzucato, Mariana (2013). *The Entrepreneurial State: Debunking Public vs. Private Myths in Risk and Innovation*. Anthem Press.

Mazzucato, Mariana (2015). 'The Green Entrepreneurial State'. *SPRU Working Paper Series*.

Mazzucato, Mariana (2016). 'From Market Fixing to Market-creating: A New Framework for Innovation Policy'. *Industry and Innovation*, Vol 23, pp 140–156.

Mazzucato, Mariana and Perez, Carlota (2014). 'Innovation as Growth Policy: The Challenge for Europe'. *SPRU Working Paper* Series. No 13.

Mazzucato, Mariana and Semieniuk, Gregor (2018). 'Financing Renewable Energy: Who is Financing What and Why it Matters'. *Technological Forecasting and Social Change*. 127, 8–22.

Mazzucato, Mariana and Wray, L. Randall (2015). 'Financing the Capital Development of the Economy: A Keynes-Schumpeter-Minsky Synthesis'. *Levy Economics Institute Working Paper*, No 837.

McGregor, J. Allister (2007). 'Researching Human Wellbeing: From Concepts to Methodology' (Working Paper 20). Retrieved from University of Bath website: http://www.bath.ac.uk/soc-pol/welldev/research/workingpaperpdf/wed20.pdf

McGregor, J. Allister (2018). 'Reconciling Universal Frameworks and Local Realities in Understanding and Measuring Wellbeing'. In: I. Bache & K. Scott (Eds.), *The Politics of Wellbeing: Theory, Policy and Practice* (pp197–224). New York: Palgrave Macmillan.

McLeod, Keith (2018). 'Our People – Multidimensional Wellbeing in New Zealand', *New Zealand Treasury Analytical Paper* (18/04), December.

Miret, Marta; Caballero, Francisco Félix; Olaya, Beatriz; Koskinen, Seppo; Naidoo, Nirmala; Tobiasz-Adamczyk, Beata; Leonardi, Matilde; Haro, Josep Maria; Chatterji, Somnath; Ayuso-Mateos, José Luis (2017). 'Association of experienced and evaluative well-being with health in nine countries with different income levels: a cross-sectional study', *Globalization and Health*, 13:65.

Morpurgo, Sir Michael (2020). 'Covid-19 will leave us a kinder world', Radio New Zealand *Sunday Morning* Interview with Jim Mora. 5 April.

Narayan, Deepa; Chambers, Robert; Shah, Meera K.; and Petesch, Patti (2000). *Voices of the poor: Crying Out for Change*. New York: Oxford University Press for The World Bank. doi:10.1596/0-1952-1602-4

National Research Council (2012). *Disaster Resilience: A National Imperative*. Washington, DC: The National Academies Press.

New Zealand Government (2019). *Wellbeing Budget 2019*. Wellington.

New Zealand Treasury (2019). *The Treasury's CBA(x) Tool*. https://treasury.govt.nz/information-and-services/state-sector-leadership/investment-management/plan-investment-choices/cost-benefit-analysis-including-public-sector-discount-rates/treasurys-cbax-tool

New Zealand Treasury (2019).
- The Start of a Conversation on the Value of New Zealand's Human Capital
- The Start of a Conversation on the Value of New Zealand's Natural Capital
- The Start of a Conversation on the Value of New Zealand's Social Capital
- The Start of a Conversation on the Value of New Zealand's Financial/Physical Capital

Nikolaev, Boris and Bennett, Daniel L. (2016). 'Give Me Liberty and Give Me Control: Economic Freedom, Control Perceptions and the Paradox of Choice'. *European Journal of Political Economy*, 45, 39–52.

Nordhaus, William D. and Tobin, James (1972). 'Is Growth Obsolete?' in *Economic Research: Retrospect and Prospect*, Volume 5, Economic Growth. NBER (pp1–80).

North, Douglas C. (1990). *Institutions, Institutional Change and Economic Performance*. Cambridge: Cambridge University Press.

North, Douglass C. (1991). 'Institutions', Journal of Economic Perspectives. Vol. 5 (1), pp97–112.

North, Douglass C. (1994). 'Economic Performance through Time'. *The American Economic Review*, 84, 359–368.

Nurse, Sir Paul (2020). "Radio New Zealand Interview with Jim Mora on his book *'What is Life?'*" Sunday, 15 November.

Nussbaum, Martha C (1999). *Sex and Social Justice*. Oxford University Press.

Nussbaum, Martha C (2000). *Women and Human Development*. Cambridge University Press.

OECD (2017 a). *OECD Economic Surveys – New Zealand*. Paris.

OECD (2017 b). *How's Life?* – https://www.keepeek.com//Digital-Asset-Management/oecd/economics/how-s-life-2017_how_life-2017-en#.Wpu1EuhubD4

OECD (2019 a). *OECD Economic Surveys – New Zealand*. Paris.

References

OECD (2019 b) *Putting Well-being Metrics into Policy Action*. International Workshop (2–4 October 2019), Paris.

OECD (2020 a). *How's Life 2020: Measuring Well-being*. Paris.

OECD (2020 b). *Measuring Well-being and Progress: Well-being research*. https://www.oecd.org/statistics/measuring-well-being-and-progress.htm

OECD (2020 c). *How's Life in New Zealand?* https://www.oecd.org/statistics/Better-Life-Initiative-country-note-New-Zealand.pdf

Olson, Mancur, Jr (1971). *The Logic of Collective Action – Public Goods and the Theory of Groups*. Harvard Economic Studies.

Ortiz-Ospina, Esteban and Roser, Max (2016) 'Trust', *Our World in Data*. University of Oxford.

Ostrom, Elinor (2009). 'Beyond Markets and States: Polycentric Governance of Complex Economic Systems', Nobel Prize Lecture. Stockholm.

Palmer, Geoffrey and Butler, Andrew (2016). *Towards Democratic Renewal: ideas for constitutional change in New Zealand*. Wellington, New Zealand: Victoria University Press.

Pelenc, Jérôme; Ballet, Jérôme; and Dedeurwaerdere, Tom (2015). 'Weak Sustainability versus Strong Sustainability'. Brief for GSDR United Nations.

Pervaiz, Zahid and Chaudhary, Amatul R. (2015). 'Social Cohesion and Economic Growth: An Empirical Investigation'. *Australian Economic Review*, 48, 369–381.

Piketty, Thomas (2017). *Capital in the 21st Century*. Harvard University Press.

Porter, Michael E.; Stern, Scott; and Green, Michael (2014). *Social Progress Index*. Washington: Social Progress Imperative.

Qasim, Mukhtar; Oxley, Les; and McLaughlin, E. (2018). 'Genuine savings as a test of New Zealand weak sustainability', *Environment, Development and Sustainability*.

Rajan, Raghuram (2019). The Third Pillar – the Revival of Community in a Polarised World. William Collins.

Rajan, Raghuram (2020). 'Thomas Piketty's "Capital and Ideology": scholarship without solutions', *Financial Times*, March 2020.

Rašković, Matevž (2020). 'How to tame "wicked problems" like Covid-19', *Newsroom*. 12 April.

Ravallion, Martin (2020). 'On the Origins of the Idea of Ending Poverty', *NBER Working Paper Series*. Working Paper 27808; September.

Rawls, John (1971). *A Theory of Justice*. Cambridge, Massachusetts: Belknap Press.

Reddy, Sanjay G. (2020). 'Coronavirus and the Limits of Economics', *Foreign Policy*. 31 March.

Reid, Chelsey (2019). *Complexity in Wellbeing and the 'Leave No-One Behind' Agenda – Studies in Aotearoa New Zealand*. Masters' of Development Studies Thesis. School of Geography, Environment and Earth Sciences. Victoria University of Wellington, New Zealand.

Robertson, Grant (2019). *2019 Budget Policy Statement*. Wellington: New Zealand Government.

Rockström, Johan; Steffen, Will; Noone, Kevin; Persson, Åsa; Chapin III, F. Stuart; Lambin, Eric; Lenton, Timothy M.; Scheffer, Marten; Folke, Carl; Schellnhuber, Hans Joachim; Nykvist, Björn; de Wit, Cynthia A.; Hughes, Terry; van der Leeuw, Sander; Rodhe, Henning; Sörlin, Sverker; Snyder, Peter K.; Costanza, Robert; Svedin, Uno; Falkenmark, Malin; Karlberg, Louise; Corell, Robert W.; Fabry, Victoria J.; Hansen, James; Walker, Brian; Liverman, Diana; Richardson, Katherine; Crutzen, Paul; and Foley, Jonathan (2009). 'Planetary Boundaries: Exploring the Safe Operating Space for Humanity'. *Ecology and Society* 14(2): 32. [online] URL: http://www.ecologyandsociety.org/vol14/iss2/art32/

Rodríguez-Pose, Andrés and von Berlepsch, Viola (2019). 'Does Population Diversity Matter for Economic Development in the Very Long-Term? Historic Migration, Diversity and County Wealth in the US'. *European Journal of Population*, 35, 873–911.

Rodrik, Dani (2004). 'Getting Institutions Right'. *CESifo DICE Report* 2, 10–15.

Rodrik, Dani (2020). 'Will Covid-19 Remake the World?' *Project Syndicate*. 6 April.

Roubini, Nouriel (2020). 'The Coming Greater Depression of the 2020s', *Project Syndicate*. 28 April.

Rovelli, Carlo (2020). *There are Places in the World where Rules are Less Important than Kindness*. Penguin.

Sachs, Jeffrey D. (2015). 'Investing in Social Capital' in J. F. Helliwell, R. Layard, J. D. Sachs (eds). *World Happiness Report*. United Nations Sustainable Solutions Network (pp152–166).

Sager, Lutz (2017). 'Income inequality and carbon consumption: Evidence from environmental Engel curves'. *Technical Report*: Grantham Research Institute on Climate Change and the Environment. No 285, November.

References

Sanger, David E.; Lipton, Eric; Sullivan, Eileen; Crowley, Michael (2020). 'Before Virus Outbreak, a Cascade of Warnings Went Unheeded', *The New York Times*. 22 March.

Santos, Laurie (2020). *The Science of Wellbeing*. Yale Lectures. https://www.coursera.org/learn/the-science-of-well-being

Saunders, Caroline and Dalziel, Paul (2017). 'Twenty-five Years of Counting for Nothing: Waring's Critique of National Accounts'. *Feminist Economics*, 23, 200–218.

Scott, James C. (1998). *Seeing Like a State: How Certain Schemes to Improve the Human Condition Have Failed*. New Haven: Yale University Press.

Schmidt, Peter (2015). *Market failure versus system failure as a rationale for economic policy? A critique from an evolutionary perspective*. Technical Report. Papers on Economics and Evolution #1504. Philipps-University, Marburg.

Scott, Karen (2012). *Measuring Wellbeing: Towards Sustainability?* New York: Routledge

Sen, Amartya K. (1996). 'On the Foundations of Welfare Economics: Utility, Capability and Practical Reason' in F. Farina, F. Hahn, and S. Vannucci (eds.), *Ethics, Rationality and Economic Behaviour* (pp50–65). Oxford: Clarendon Press.

Sen, Amartya K. (1999). *Development as Freedom*. New York: Oxford University Press.

Sen, Amartya K. (2009). *The Idea of Justice*. Cambridge. Belknap.

Sen, Amartya K. (2017). *Collective Choice and Social Welfare*. Penguin Books.

Smith, Conal (2015). 'Measuring Well-being: Progress to Date and Remaining Challenges', *KDI School, Sejong* OECD Presentation Slides; 24 November.

Smith, Conal (2018). 'TacklingPovertyNZ – the nature of poverty in New Zealand and ways to address it', *Policy Quarterly*. Victoria University of Wellington. Volume 14(1), February.

Soros, George (2003). *The Alchemy of Finance*. New Jersey: Wiley.

Spolaore, Enrico and Wacziarg, Romain (2013). 'How Deep are the Roots of Economic Development?' *Journal of Economic Literature*, 51, 325–369.

Stephenson, Janet (2020). 'Covid-19 has nothing on what's coming', *Newsroom*. 20 April.

Stiglitz, Joseph E.; Sen, Amartya K.; Fitoussi, Jean-Paul (2009). *Report by the Commission on the Measurement of Economic Performance and Social Progress*. Paris: Commission on the Measurement of Economic Performance and Social Progress.

Stoel, Maaike (2019). 'The Monitor of Well-being and the Integration of the Dutch Policy Cycle'. Presentation at the OECD international workshop on *Putting Well-being Metrics into Policy Action* (2–4 October 2019), Paris.

Stutzer, Alois (2019). 'Happiness and Public Policy: A Procedural Perspective', *IZA Institute of Labor Economics Discussion Paper Series*. IZA DP No. 12622. September.

Tcherneva, Pavlina (2020). 'What would Franklin D. Roosevelt do?', *Project Syndicate*. 24 March.

Tirole, Jean (2017). *Economics for the Common Good*. Princeton University Press.

Tobgay, Tshering (2016). 'This country is not just carbon neutral – it is carbon negative', TED Talks. 11 March.

Toledo, Alejandro (2016). 'Eradicating Poverty, Reducing Inequality, and Promoting Sustainable Development'. Papers presented at global meetings of the emerging markets forum.

Trotter, Chris (2020). 'Chris Trotter argues if Jacinda Ardern is able to successfully lead New Zealand through the coronavirus pandemic the Labour Party might finally be able to shake-off the neoliberal monkey on its back', *interest.co.nz*, 16 March.

Tourism Industry Aotearoa (2020). *Press Release*. Scoop Independent News. 8 April.

United Arab Emirates (2017) *Happiness Policy Manual*. https://government.ae/en/about-the-uae/the-uae-government/government-of-future/happiness

United Nations Development Programme (UNDP) (2019). *Sustainable Development Goals*. United Nations, New York.

United States Declaration of Independence (1776). *The Declaration of Independence* – Full Text: USHistory.org. https://www.ushistory.org/declaration/document/

Van den Bergh, Jeroen C.J.M. (2009). 'The GDP Paradox', *Journal of Economic Psychology*. 30(2), 117-135.

Vásquez, Ian and Porčnik, Tanja (2019). *The Human Freedom Index 2019 – A Global Measurement of Personal, Civil, and Economic Freedom*. CATO Institute.

References

Wallace, Jennifer (2019). 'What can Scotland, Wales, and Northern Ireland tell us about the role of legislation in promoting societal wellbeing?' Presentation at the OECD international workshop on *Putting Well-being Metrics into Policy Action* (2–4 October 2019), Paris.

Walzer, Michael (1983). *Spheres of Justice: A Defense of Pluralism and Equality*. New York: Basic Book.

Waring, Marilyn (1988). *If Women Counted: A New Feminist Economics*. San Francisco: Harper & Row.

Warren, Ken (2019). 'Designing a new Collective Operating and Funding Model in the New Zealand Public Sector', DRAFT *New Zealand Treasury Working Paper*, December.

Winkler, Othmar W. (2009). *Interpreting Economic and Social Data – A Foundation of Descriptive Statistics*. Springer.

Wellmon, Chad (2020). 'The Scholar's Vocation', *Aeon Newsletter*. 8 April.

Welsch, Heinz and Biermann, Philipp (2017). 'Poverty is a Public Bad: Panel Evidence from Subjective Wellbeing Data'. *The Review of Income and Wealth*. November https://doi.org/10.1111/roiw.12350

Wendling, Zachary A.; Emerson, John W.; Esty, Daniel C.; Levy, Marc A.; de Sherbinin, Alex, *et al.* (2018). *2018 Environmental Performance Index*. New Haven, CT: Yale Center for Environmental Law & Policy. https://epi.yale.edu/

White, Sarah C. (2010). 'Analysing wellbeing: a framework for development practice'. *Development in Practice*, 20(2), 158–172. doi:10.1080/09614520903564199

Wikipedia (I = PAT). *I=PAT*.

Wikipedia (2020). *Ministry of Works and Development*.

Williamson, Oliver E. (2000). 'The New Institutional Economics: Taking Stock, Looking Ahead', *Journal of Economic Literature*. Vol. XXXVIII (September), pp595–613.

Winkler, Othmar W. (2009). *Interpreting Economic and Social Data – A Foundation of Descriptive Statistics*. Springer.

Yamamura, Eiji (2016). 'Social Conflict and Redistributive Preferences among Pich and poor: Testing the Hypothesis of Acemoglu and Robinson'. *Journal of Applied Economics*, 19, 41–63.

About the author

Dr Girol Karacaoglu BA MBA Bogazici, PhD Hawaii
Professor of Policy Practice, Victoria University of Wellington

Girol Karacaoglu is the Head of School of Government at Victoria University of Wellington (VUW). He came to VUW from the New Zealand Treasury, where he was Chief Economist. Before then, he was the Chief Executive of PSIS (then Co-operative Bank of New Zealand) for nine years.

His previous roles included General Manager at Westpac New Zealand, Chief Economist at the National Bank of New Zealand, and lecturer in Economics at Victoria University of Wellington.

His academic fields of specialisation were in Monetary and Financial Economics, International Finance, Econometrics, Corporate Accounting and Finance. His current research interest is in public policy: an integrated approach to environmental, social, and economic policies towards improving intergenerational wellbeing.

Thanks

In 2012, just before I joined the New Zealand Treasury, I read, and got very excited about, the potential offered for public policy advice, of an early version of a paper written by Ben Gleisner and colleagues at the Treasury ('A living standards approach to public policy making') which was eventually published in the *New Zealand Economic Papers* in 2012.

As the story goes, the earlier version of that paper was written, at the request of the then Treasury Secretary John Whitehead, who wanted to understand and explore the implications of the now famous Stiglitz, Sen, and Fitoussi (2009) *Report by the Commission on the Measurement of Economic Performance and Social Progress*, for public policy in New Zealand.

At the time I joined the Treasury, Gabriel Makhlouf (Gabs) was the Treasury Secretary. That period was dominated by three major and interrelated themes – developing a multi-disciplinary framework for the formulation of public policy advice, building on that earlier 'living standards' paper; diversity and inclusion; and system leadership.

A multidisciplinary approach demands no compromise in what each discipline contributes to public policy formulation, but creates the ecosystem that allows – in fact embraces – the diversity of perspectives that they each offer. The role of leadership then is to provide the environment where that diversity is nourished, and somehow integrated, as a platform for advice to improve the lives of people on a sustainable basis.

Gabs was strongly of the view that, if we wanted to lead change in the public policy domain to effectively address the myriad of wicked problems we were surrounded with, we had to first change the conversation. Simply doing policy-informing research and publishing the fruits of that research through a set of technical papers, would not suffice.

Gabs and our colleagues at the senior management team provided the environment and support for some of us to pursue that multidisciplinary public-policy informing research, while they tried to change the conversation by promoting the Living Standards Framework as a platform for policy advice in their public and official engagements.

About the author

I owe a lot to Gabs and my Treasury colleagues, including Margaret Galt, Ken Warren, and one of my co-authors for the initial (more technical) version of the present book, Anita King, for their encouragement and support. And, of course, to my second co-author for that same book (Jacek Krawczyk) from whom I learned a great deal over the past eight years.

The School of Government at Victoria University of Wellington provided the academic environment where I could imbed my interest in wellbeing and public policy into my reading, research, conversations, and teaching. Among my colleagues, Jonathan Boston's work on governing for the future had a lot of influence on my thinking. So did the work of my students, such as Chelsey Reid. They introduced me to literature, and ways of thinking, outside of the domain of economics, that I was not familiar with.

Finally, Angela, my wife, provided a peaceful and comfortable place for me, to enjoy my reading and writing.

I owe thanks to all of them.

💚 Supporting The Nest Collective

Half of the net revenue from sales of this book will be donated to The Nest Collective, which gives baby and children's essentials to families in need.

A collective of volunteers across Aotearoa, they work alongside social workers to ensure families are supported in their parenting journey, gifting new, pre-loved, handcrafted and repurposed essentials, including clothing, bedding, books and much, much more.

The Nest Collective believe that together we can make a real difference for the families who need it most. Their soon-to-be-launched website will be at:

https://thenestcollective.org.nz

About the publisher

FINDING MEANING IN A DIFFICULT WORLD

A word in *te reo Maori* tuwhiri means to disclose, reveal, divulge, make known, or a clue, a means of discovering or disclosing something lost or hidden, a hint, a tip, a pointer. The Tuwhiri Project has arisen out of the development of a secular Buddhism, a trend in contemporary western Buddhism which highlights the fundamental ethic of the teachings of Gotama, the historical Buddha – *care* – in all its aspects. Secularity calls on us to express this ethic of care in ways appropriate to our time and current predicaments.

While humanity may well come to grips with the current pandemic in the foreseeable future, ballooning inequalities and injustice threaten to shred the fabric of our societies, and the climate emergency menaces all life forms on the planet.

In the face of these enduring humanity-induced catastrophes, we owe a special duty of care to future generations to overcome them, and to leave our successors with a safer, fairer world in which they may thrive. We need to express our care for coming generations in many ways, from changing our own personal lifestyles, to choosing political representatives who advance cogent, long-sighted policies in aid of a better world.

This book makes no claim to Buddhist inspiration. However, it directly serves the Buddhist ethic of care in advocating coherent socioeconomic policies that will benefit people alive today, and those who will succeed us. For this reason Tuwhiri takes great pleasure in publishing it. To find out how you can support The Tuwhiri Project, please go to:

https://tuwhiri.nz/about

www.ingramcontent.com/pod-product-compliance
Lightning Source LLC
Chambersburg PA
CBHW051358290426
44108CB00015B/2059